Rediscovering the Jesus Story: A Participatory Guide

Joseph A. Grassi

PAULIST PRESS
New York/Mahwah, NJ

Library of Congress Cataloging-in-Publication Data

Grassi, Joseph A.
    Rediscovering the Jesus story : a participatory guide / Joseph A. Grassi.
        p. cm.
    Includes bibliographical references.
    ISBN 0-8091-3589-2 (alk. paper)
    1. Jesus Christ—Biography—Study and teaching.   2. Jesus Christ—Teachings—Study and teaching. 3. Jesus Christ—Person and offices—Study and teaching. 4. Bible. N.T. Gospels—Criticism, interpretation, etc. 5. Bible. N.T. Gospels—Study and teaching. I. Title.
BT301.2.G685   1995
226'.06—dc20
                                                                        95-22277
                                                                        CIP

Published by Paulist Press
997 Macarthur Boulevard
Mahwah, NJ 07430

Printed and bound in the
United States of America

Contents

Introduction

The joys of *discovery* are among the greatest of human existence. They have a first-time quality about them, whether it is a child seeing a sunset for the first time or an adult finding a new friend. But as time goes on, our minds become cluttered with preoccupations, concerns and worries. These make us gradually lose the beauties of those first moments; we then feel the need to go back and *rediscover*. The same has happened with the gospels, originally written as good news to promote the joys of discovering the Jesus story in a very personal way.

Why the need to "rediscover" the Jesus story? Don't we already have it in the text of Jesus' first biographers, Matthew, Mark, Luke and John? The answer lies in the etymology of the word "discover," which means to remove some kind of impeding "cover." Over the past two thousand years there has been a progressive thickening of two principal covers that function like a cloud over the sun. A cloud lets in the minimum light we need but keeps us from experiencing the full warmth, energy and brilliant display of color that pure sunlight provides.

What are the obstacles that impede a full meaningful discovery of the Jesus story in the gospels? The first of these is the gradual loss of many necessary clues to meaning that the early gospel audience possessed, but most modern audiences do not have. The most important of these lost keys is the knowledge and familiarity with the Hebrew/Jewish scriptures possessed by ancient audiences. This familiarity was the lifeblood of every Jew, including Jesus himself and most of the gospel writers. Even non-Jewish converts to Christianity had this background because their pre-gospel training took place through careful reading and study of these scriptures.

What difference would ignorance of these scriptures make? Let us contrast a modern newspaper story to the gospels. A news reader today wants all the lurid details the imagination can possibly capture. However, the gospel writers were interested in much more than factual details; they wanted to bring out the *meaning* of Jesus' life. The evangelists had to explain this meaning in terms of the scriptures. Why? Because they believed that the scriptures were inspired by God and contained the powerful divine plan for the world that Jesus was trying to bring to completion. Many gospel stories are a careful weaving together of scriptural references to make this evident. The loss of the Hebrew/Jewish scripture background is the loss of a vital key to discovering the Jesus story.

The second heavy lid to be dis-covered is the loss of appreciation and application of the gospels as *dramatic narrative*. Recovery of this factor is among the greatest contributions of modern scholarship. This recovery is essential; over the centuries, the inner drama of the gospels has become cluttered by intensive use of these stories as sources of information, fact-finding and sometimes even dogmas about Jesus. This has resulted in some scholars even setting themselves up as possessing a privileged monopoly on understanding the gospels.

The expression "dramatic narrative" is not just another phrase of scholarly lingo. A similar example today would be a good play, opera or movie. People today would quickly abandon crowded movie halls if they knew they had to attend classes or lectures to find out the meaning of what they have seen and heard, and worse still if they needed to take notes during performances or take an exam afterward!

What are the characteristics of dramatic narrative? Here are some:

1) A definite plot from beginning to end. We cannot "stop the show" and understand any part in isolation. Each part contributes to the whole and the whole is found in each part. Thus, in the Jesus story each incident must be understood in light of the total effect his triumphant death and resurrection had on such events. Every story-event moves toward this.

2) Characters in the plot that an audience can identify with. Drama is not limited to an historical time period. People laugh or cry, experience joy or fear as they identify with characters in

the drama of their own life experience. In the Jesus story, the impulsive Peter cries after denying three times that he even knew Jesus at all. We identify with him as we realize that few of us could have done worse, yet Jesus made him the founding rock of his community. This suggests we can have a fresh start in life no matter what the past has been.

Connected with #2 is #3, the *rhetorical* nature of drama. This means they persuade and move people totally and emotionally to go ahead in life with new courage, energy and hope. They are not mere sources of "ancient history" by providing facts or information for discussions or classes that eventually may prove to be dull and boring. A modern audience goes to a movie or drama to obtain a valuable personal experience, whether it be entertainment or new insights into their life. How do performances obtain a one, two, three or four star rating? It is all based on the extent to which they involve the audience in a long remembered deep personal experience.

4) Dramatic narrative lends itself to considerable diversity of meaning as each person in the audience undergoes a unique personal experience through its medium. That is why we usually like to go to a drama with someone else so we can share afterward this diversity of experience. We rarely find two people who completely agree. It is true that the author/composer has some overriding purpose in mind but he or she cannot dictate what effect it is to have on each person. In fact, all the beautiful harmony of the universe is made possible through the wonderful diversity in all of nature, especially human beings. True *oneness* comes about through recognition of diversity. False "unity," through uniformity and destruction of diversity, promotes slavery and dictatorships.

5) Enhancing the dramatic quality of the gospels is the fact that *relatively few people actually read the gospels in early centuries.* Handwritten scrolls or codices (page-type manuscripts) required long tedious hours of hand copy work and were expensive and difficult to obtain. In addition, reading and writing were often skills possessed by a small minority. So for centuries the gospels retained their *performance* quality. Skillful performers read and even acted out the gospel text using every possible technique to capture and excite their audiences. The

frequent use of the words *hear* or *listen* in the gospels stimulated the audience to keep alert and really take in the message.

The gospels, in the best sense of the word, were also *live performances.* They did not consider Jesus as a dead person of the distant past but as present *here and now* to believers. The actual person narrating the gospel was only a channel or instrument of Jesus' actual words. Jesus was speaking to them with all the dynamic power and effect that he had on his audiences years or centuries ago in Galilee. The gospel audience heard his words not merely in terms of valuable information but also as empowerment and energy to accomplish the things they heard. The stories of miracles, healings, and forgiveness were only reminders that the same events were now happening again through Jesus' presence in their midst.

In our own times there is a mania for fast food, instant information and rapid reading. Why read something again if you get it the first time? However, in oral dramatic transmission, the focus is on depth, not territory covered. As a result a continual sharpening of listening powers is essential. Dramatic repetition is very important so people will remember the message and put it into practice. Therefore, audiences would listen repeatedly to the same gospel for further depth, empowerment and new insights. Even today, the best test of the quality of any drama or movie is the desire an audience has to see it again.

THE BIG QUESTION IS: HOW WILL THIS BOOK REALLY HELP TO DISCOVER THE GOSPELS ANEW? 1) Our purpose is to lead into the gospel text, not out of it. References to your own New Testament text will be in bold type as well as the headings for each gospel story. 2) Following each story, you will find the necessary background a modern audience needs to *discover* the gospel anew. One example of this is the essential background of the Jewish/Hebrew scriptures along with guides to the meaning of each story within each gospel's dramatic and literary pattern. There will be cross-references to other gospels for additional information. 3) At the end of each "chapter" (chapter and verse numbers were added centuries later) or section the reader will find *Pathways to Further Discovery.* This will consist of suggested paths to study and discover more about the evangelists' dramatic sequences. Then there will be suggestions for keeping a personal journal as you study the gospels. All of the above will be suggestions toward making the journey of Jesus in the gospels your own journey as well. The Jesus story really has little meaning unless it becomes linked to each individual's personal story.

This book is especially oriented toward use as an advanced high school or a college text. It will also be very helpful for discussion groups or personal exploration.

PART I
THE JESUS STORY:
THE VOICE OF MARK

Introduction to Mark

Mark originally wrote his gospel close to the time of the Jewish war with Rome, around 66–70 A.D., and the destruction of the Jewish temple. This was a period of painful crisis for both Jews and Christians alike. Rome was the unchallenged master of the world at that time. Mark wrote for believers facing a terrible burden of abusive Roman authority in their daily lives. This was either directly under greedy Roman governors or under sometimes worse puppets of Rome. Failure to stand up for what you believed in could result in arrest, persecution, imprisonment or even death.

Christians had agonizing choices to make. One alternative was to admit that they were just plain "losers" trying to confront Rome, the greatest "winner" the world had ever known. In practice this meant to just go along with what government asked of them, even if it compromised their consciences. A second alternative was to follow some Christian teachers who claimed that a great final battle between the forces of good and evil was very soon to take place. When all hope seemed lost, Jesus would suddenly return from heaven with great power and miracles. He would crush the believers' oppressors, relieve their sufferings, open their prisons and win a great victory over Rome despite impossible obstacles.

A third alternative, that of this gospel, was to follow Jesus in his faithfulness to what he believed even if it led to suffering

1

and the cross. Perhaps discouragement was the greatest temptation of those who chose this alternative. Jesus had called them to be fishers for people. Yet what could one or a few people do to make a real impression on the hardened Roman military?

Does this audience situation mean anything today? A sincere believer still faces a terrible sense of helplessness in dealing with a world of so much crime, violence, war and injustice. Is it worthwhile to stand up for values if it only means continually being knocked down and being regarded as a real loser? What good can a few people really accomplish? Can I hope to make a difference to a vast world dominated by so much evil?

This gospel tells how Jesus faced the same temptations and feeling of hopelessness. It tells how he learned to win by being willing to be considered a loser by others. This gospel is a do-it-yourself guide for people to obtain the same resources as Jesus and to do the same things that he did. Only in this way can you have a real impact on people around you.

You might wonder if this gospel is only for Christians of Jewish origin or for everyone. It is for everyone. So the writer takes pains to explain Jewish customs and translate Aramaic (the Hebrew-related language of Jesus) into the Greek used in the gospel. Mark has a broad universal orientation. His purpose is to show how Jesus, originally a Jewish messiah, has meaning for all people of all time.

SUGGESTIONS FOR STUDY:

Before starting, read (aloud if possible) the entire gospel of Mark in one or two sittings. This is necessary because each episode does not stand by itself. As dramatic narrative, each story has meaning in light of the whole story of Jesus. Not to do this would be like returning to a movie for ten minute sections each week!

The Gospel According to Mark

The Proclamation of John the Baptist

1:1 The **good news** (gospel) celebrates a new great intervention of God in the world that people can experience through **Jesus** (his earthly Greek name, from the root *save*). He is the long awaited **Christ**, a Greek translation of the Hebrew *messiah*, meaning, "anointed one." This was God's chosen agent whom the people of Israel hoped would come to initiate a new age in the world. The whole gospel will be devoted to explain the secret meaning of the title, **Son of God**.

The inauguration of a new president must be announced to the whole world and invitations sent out. So also, God's inauguration of his new rule on earth needs a chosen messenger to **prepare the way**. This is **John the Baptist** who appears in the **wilderness** (desert), which symbolizes crisis, temptation and fresh beginnings. The desert theme traces back to Israel's temptation in the Sinai desert on the way to the promised land. The **river Jordan** is the river of new beginnings that the people crossed to enter the new land. All this emphasizes the new beginnings and new life that are open for people. It means breaking old life patterns and becoming a child/youth once more through a **baptism of repentance**. Baptism is literally a "plunging into." The break with the heavy guilt and burden of the past comes through a full **forgiveness of sins**. However it is necessary to acknowledge and take responsibility for one's life, so Mark emphasizes that the people were **confessing their sins**.

Notice that **John was clothed with camel's hair, with a**

3

leather belt. This garb is like that of Elijah the prophet in 2 Kings 1:8. This makes the important point that John the Baptist is the chosen messenger of God announced in the last words of the last biblical prophet Malachi: **Lo, I will send you the prophet Elijah before the great and terrible day of the Lord** (4:1). The "great and terrible day" is the time of God's promised powerful future intervention in the world. The Baptist and then Jesus announce that this day is at hand for the gospel audience when they really listen to the message and take it into their hearts.

He will baptize you with the Holy Spirit. This introduces the next story of Jesus' immersion in the Spirit so he can be its source to others. In the bible, God's life-giving presence in all creation is called the *Spirit*. But here the *Holy* Spirit emphasizes the moral transforming role of this Spirit. Jesus will possess this so fully that he will baptize/plunge others into sharing this unique gift.

The Baptism of Jesus

1:9 This story is not only for those soon to be baptized but to recall to those already baptized the meaning of this supreme event. It is not a religious rite from the distant past but a new beginning repeatedly experienced. Jesus descended into the Jordan's muddy waters along with "sinners," people of all walks of life, to provide a model for imitation. No person can ever look down on others in an air of superiority, but must undergo a continual conversion each day. Jesus' awareness of a **dove** descending on him was the sign of a great interior experience of the Spirit that God called him to share with others. The secret interior words from God, **You are my Son**, designated an intimate relationship to God as Father. This was not primarily in a masculine sense but in the deepest sense of a child-to-parent relationship of complete devotion.

The Temptation of Jesus

1:13 When an inner call comes from God like that of Jesus, it signals difficult choices, for that is what temptation means. **Satan** is the embodiment of all the powers of evil in the world that people must face. The story is brief at this point because the whole gospel is Jesus' story of courageous conflict with evil. Yet evil is not simply a disaster but a test, opportunity and challenge to respond and overcome through the tremendous power of the Spirit within. Not to respond or to remain neutral is to cooperate in evil.

The Beginning of the Galilean Ministry

1:14 **After John was arrested**. The Baptist soon became embroiled in trouble because of his courageous stand in confronting moral injustice (see particulars in 6:17–29). As a colleague of John, Jesus felt the shadow of imprisonment and death fall upon him if he continued John's work of preaching. Yet despite this he went bravely ahead. In fact, God's message was so important and urgent for him that he took the ultimate risk by going beyond John: He left the narrow valley of the Jordan and went up to Galilee to reach a broader public. John had waited for people to come down to him in repentance. Jesus in contrast took the initiative to go up to people where they were and invite them even at home or at their jobs. Jesus' first recorded words, the perennial message of God addressed to readers, were **The time is fulfilled and the kingdom of God has come near; repent and believe in the good news**.

Jesus Calls His First Disciples

1:16 In this story we find the meaning of a call to discipleship. Simon and his brother Andrew are primary examples. Jesus says to us as audience: **I will make you fish for people**. In other words, the mission is to really change the world and bring people to God. This seems so impossible and overpowering that Jesus emphasizes that there is no need to trust in only human strength: "**I will make you** fish for people." One of the greatest privileges of life is to recognize that each one of us has some particular gift that can make a real impact on the world. However, special privilege requires special response and responsibility, so the disciples in the gospel story **left all and followed him**. This does not mean giving up a means of livelihood although it may mean so for a time as it did for the first apostles. It does mean a total priority for the **kingdom of God** (15). This "kingdom" is a world where God truly rules, a world of peace, justice and love. The call has priority over family, friends and careers, so Mark notes, **Immediately he called them and they left their father Zebedee in the boat with the hired men and followed him**.

Confidence

The Exorcism in the Synagogue

1:21 The call to discipleship is dangerous and risky. Confidence is necessary to win a hard-fought battle against the overwhelming forces of evil. So the gospel assures readers of Jesus' power to do so, a resource that they will share also (6:7–13). An **unclean spirit** was considered a demon that makes people "unclean." This does not mean "dirty" but a condition that disqualifies a person from taking part in certain religious rituals or community functions. In an age that did not know about germs and viruses (which are living beings!), the ancients attributed illness to living organisms within, a demon that made people "unclean." It is important to realize that Jesus has power over every outside controlling force, even those threatening the holiest of places, the synagogue. (On "demons" see comments on Matthew 6:13.) So the people (audience) in the gospel story are **amazed** by Jesus' **new teaching** and **authority**.

Jesus Heals Simon's Mother-in-Law

1:29 Simon's house at Capernaum, by the lake of Galilee, became Jesus' headquarters after his home town of Nazareth (6:1–6) rejected him. According to custom, the mother of Simon's wife supervised the household, especially in matters of food and hospitality. Like the disciples, people can tell Jesus about those who are in need of help. Notice how Jesus cures through personal contact and touch. The goal of a cure is restoration to normal life and work. For Simon's mother-in-law, this was to **serve them**, meaning her household but now including Jesus and his hungry disciples. This story begins a cycle of stories about women in this gospel who will later take on a surprising new role.

Jesus' Prayer Before a Galilean Preaching Tour

1:35 The disciples awaken one morning only to find their popular teacher is missing. They finally locate him praying by himself in a deserted spot. They press him to return to action, for crowds of people are waiting to see him. However, Jesus is not a workaholic or a non-stop activist, and he shows how necessary prayer and solitude are for a fruitful active life. His disciples want him to capitalize on his popularity and become a local leader. However his special purpose is to spread the good news to as many as possible, not to develop a local following. This will be the gift of others; he must be faithful to a wider call. Jesus' message is to trust in our own special gifts to do some things and to trust in the gifts of other people for what they can accomplish. Trying to be always "on stage" is self-promotion.

Jesus Cleanses and Heals a Leper

1:40 Mark could have chosen many healing stories about the master, but only selected those that seemed most impossible or paralleled and even surpassed those of the ancient scriptures. He was especially interested in those cures that highlight passages from death to life, for this is what Jesus' own death accomplished for others. Leprosy was the most fearful and deadly form of ritual uncleanness. It was so powerful that it could be caught, like a contagious disease, by touching a leper. Consequently these miserable people lived in groups outside cities, often in cemeteries to avoid contact with others. They were very much like walking corpses shunned even by their own families.

The crowds around Jesus drew back in horror when a leper came out of hiding and approached Jesus for a cure. Everyone was shocked to the core when **Jesus stretched out his hand and touched him**, thus incurring uncleanness himself according to the laws in Leviticus 13–14. Jesus ordered the man to go to the temple priests and perform the ceremonies necessary to reconsecrate him for full participation once more in community life. The message was clear that the disciples' mission was to go out to the outcasts and marginalized of the world to bring them back to full restoration. Nothing less is enough. Handouts and charity can be even demeaning without the goal of full dignity and community restoration. Jesus commanded, **See that you say nothing to anyone**. This sounds impossible but the idea is that Jesus deliberately played down his healer role to draw attention to his teaching and the total message of the gospel.

PATHWAYS TO FURTHER DISCOVERY:

1. How does the beginning of the Jesus story in 1:1–20 parallel and foreshadow the end in 15:25–16:8?

2. Jesus said, "Follow me and I will make you fish for people." In the gospel, what surprises do we find regarding the ones who will actually follow Jesus until the cross and make possible a "fishing expedition" to the world?

PERSONAL JOURNAL SUGGESTION:

The baptism story signifies breaking from old patterns of life and making new beginnings. Note in your journal each day something *new*—perhaps something you have never done before or something that has never happened to you before. Write your reactions to this experience.

Jesus Heals and Forgives a Paralytic

2:1 Mark wrote this story in so much detail to illustrate that Jesus' healing was not just external, but a cure of the whole person. This involved a complete turning to God and total forgiveness of the past. This healing and forgiving ministry is the principal sign of Jesus' presence in the world today. The essential inner ingredient to make this happen lies in the words, **When Jesus saw their faith**—a trust so great that the paralytic's friends tore a hole in a thatch roof to lower him down on ropes in front of Jesus. The scribes (professional writers and religion teachers) thought that Jesus blasphemed by assuming God's authority in judgment in saying, **Son, your**

sins are forgiven. Jesus replies that he has that authority on earth as **Son of Man**. This title can mean simply a human being.

However, an audience trained in scripture would recall the great vision of the future of the prophet Daniel (7:9–14). In the vision, God enthroned as judge gives his power and authority to one "like a Son of Man." This Son of Man is human, representing Israel, the people of God. At the same time, he is divine-like, by sharing God's judgment and authority. As Son of Man, Jesus is present in the people of God **on earth**. Therefore, the community's reception and forgiveness of others is God's own loving forgiveness as well. This removes the heavy fearful burden of future judgment. Believers can be saved from this fear here and now. This is the meaning of "salvation." Today this occurs in the community sacrament of reconciliation.

Jesus Calls Levi the Tax Collector

2:13 Mark's stories link together closely. Here we have a practical application of acceptance and forgiveness for the most unlikely prospect: Levi the tax collector. Everyone despised him as an employee of an abusive foreign power. Levi had become rich on the lifeblood of his own people. Yet the master shocked everyone by choosing Levi as a disciple. Not only that, but Jesus also surprised Levi's notorious friends by welcoming them to full community table fellowship with himself and his disciples. Forgiveness is not merely internal but communal as well.

The **Pharisees**, of course, were completely shocked. These men were respected teachers of unimpeachable integrity. They pledged themselves to perfect observance of the traditional law, even going beyond what the law required. Yet Jesus answered them, **Those who are well have no need of a physician but those who are sick**. As healing physician, Jesus can only help those who acknowledge they are sick and needy. Many Pharisees as dedicated religion teachers felt no such need. Yet Jesus stated that he had come **not to call the righteous but those who are sick**. Thus the audience paradox: when we think we are righteous and good, then we cannot be helped; when we acknowledge human weakness, then we can become healed and a follower of Jesus. The only glorious title of a Christian is that of a repentant sinner.

Is Religion Serious Fasting or Joyous Feasting?

2:18 By way of connection to the previous story, the Baptist and the Pharisees followed the traditional way of repentance; this was through self-discipline, prayer and asceticism. Jesus' way was a striking contrast. Jesus counteracted forbidden pleasures by finding more pleasure and joy, not less. So his way was like that of a joyful **wedding** celebration. The Jews then celebrated a marriage with seven full days of festivity. People put aside ordinary work and enjoyed the wine, food and entertainment lavishly provided by the wedding party. Jesus' approach is not just a **patch** on an old garment (tradition); it is sparkling **new wine** that will burst any old containers.

The Joyful Spirit of the Sabbath

2:23 The new wine motif is now applied to the holy sabbath. The third commandment enjoined the special religious observation of every Saturday. Early Christians gradually transferred this to Sunday in memory of Jesus' resurrection. Church leaders in time added other obligations such as special religious ceremonies. Jesus explains the true spirit of any law: **The sabbath was made for humankind and not humankind for the sabbath.** True religion is person-centered, not precept-centered. **The Son of Man is Lord of the sabbath.** A joyful presence of the Lord makes Sunday a day of communal joy and refreshment.

In the second sabbath story, Jesus looked at his opponents **with anger.** Throughout Mark, we find a full range of human emotions. The statements of Jesus were a real challenge to the Pharisee religion teachers and others: **The Pharisees went out and immediately conspired with the Herodians against him, how to destroy him.** Mark has this important plot indicator as foreshadowing the gospel ending. Jesus' supreme independence enrages some religion teachers who feel that Jesus is subverting religious law (which was civil law as well) and thus endangering their traditions and lifestyle. (The Herodians were supporters of King Herod of Galilee who would regard Jesus as a political threat.)

PATHWAYS TO FURTHER DISCOVERY:

Trace how the central theme of forgiveness moves through the gospel from beginning to end in very concrete ways.

PERSONAL JOURNAL SUGGESTION:

Each day, recall people you have hurt or who have hurt you in some way. Send them energy and forgiveness. If possible, plan how you could do something special for them.

Teaching and Healing by the Seashore

3:7 **Jesus departed with his disciples to the sea.** Notice the drama sequences Mark uses: 1) opposition (plot against Jesus), 2) temporary withdrawal/strategic retreat of Jesus for regathering forces, 3) renewed and expanded campaign. We could call this Jesus' one step backward, two steps forward approach. Here Jesus retreats from Capernaum to the sea where his audience widens to many more people from far-off places. To broaden his apostolate he appoints the twelve and shares his powers with them.

Jesus Appoints the Twelve

3:13 This important event foreshadows Jesus' death and the resulting expansion of his work afterward. Jacob (new name, Israel) before his death blessed his twelve sons to carry on his name and mission as the twelve tribes of Israel. Jesus also acts in a parallel manner. **So he appointed twelve; Simon (to whom he gave the name Peter).** *Petros* is the Greek word for "rock." In the bible, when God gives a new name, such as to Abram and Jacob, he gives with it a new divine and powerful mission. Jesus appoints "Rocky" as his special leader for his future mission. Jesus' one step backward, two steps forward approach is meant to be a model for the audience of any time when they face the obstacles toward making the kingdom of God a priority. The following episodes illustrate examples of this opposition.

Jesus Faces Determined Opposition

3:20 Even Jesus' family tries to restrain him. The pressing crowds kept him so busy that people were calling him a madman and fanatic. His family feared he might be arrested by Herod or Roman authority as a dangerous popular leader. This had already happened to John the Baptist. The family knew well that the Romans had crucified thousands of Jews in a revolt around the time of Jesus' birth. They were determined to do all they possibly could to keep Jesus from a similar fate.

Mark takes special note of the **scribes who had come down from Jerusalem**. This is an ominous notice of broadening opposition as important teachers from Jerusalem the capital arrive to keep Jesus under surveillance. Their attack is a subtle one on the very character of Jesus: **By the ruler of demons he casts out demons.** In other words, they are saying that Jesus is a power-hungry agent of Satan. This cruel attack is a **sin against the Holy Spirit** by turning good into evil and has serious consequences. Mark is warning his audience that "fanatic, crazy, possessed and power-hungry" are all familiar terms they may hear when they take Jesus' message seriously.

The True Family of Jesus

3:31 The hardest blows sometimes come from those closest to you. Jesus' mother and his family exert their authority by summoning Jesus to leave the crowded home where he is teaching. Sadly, Jesus has to turn to his audience then and now and say who his true family is: **Whoever does the will of God is my brother and sister and mother.** Yet this is another example of the "one step, two step" pattern. The heavy loss of home support offers the possibility of new friends and family as supporting teams for doing what God wants in the world.

PATHWAYS TO FURTHER DISCOVERY:

Find other places in the gospel where the "one step, two step" dramatic sequence is found. How does this apply to the audience?

PERSONAL JOURNAL SUGGESTION:

Apply the "one step, two step" method of Jesus to situations where you have encountered opposition or have experienced apparent failure.

Jesus Teaches in Parables: The Sower

4:1 Jesus was a master storyteller. A parable is really a masterpiece of art, an invitation of grace to find ourselves in the story when we compare God's ways and ours. Here, God is like a foolish farmer scattering enormous quantities of seed in places where it will be mostly lost—on a hardened path, on rocky ground, or soil covered with thorns and weeds. What a waste of time and effort this seems! Yet **other seed fell into good soil.** This is good, deep, receptive ground for the all-powerful seed which is **the word** of God (4:14). This yields an unbelievable harvest of **thirty- and sixty- and a hundred-fold.**

Ordinary farming at that time yielded perhaps eight or ten times as much wheat seed as that sowed. Jesus is describing a *miraculous* harvest only made possible by God. The biblical parallel is Isaac, the father of Jacob, when God blessed him to give him a **hundred-fold** harvest (Genesis 26:12). This occurred despite the opposition of Isaac's enemies and a drought in the land. The seed parables follow the opposition stories to give hope to readers of all times. There will always be some deep ground in ourselves and others to produce a miraculous harvest despite previous failures and opposition.

The Purpose of Parables

4:10 This purpose is to give people the opportunity to listen for themselves and make their own choice to be either insiders or outsiders. If they choose the latter, they cut off the opportunity to **turn again and be forgiven.** The parable explanations apply the parables to temptation, persecution and money as obstacles to growth. These explanations are the voice of Jesus which Mark does not regard as limited to one historical situation but as continually speaking to people in all times and situations.

The Lamp Under a Bushel

4:21 Mark would have smiled to know that Jesus' words have become an English proverb: "Don't hide your light under a bushel." The image was much more dramatic when using a little smoky oil lamp of centuries ago. Why is it that people are so discouraged by difficulties and opposition? It is because they withdraw within and keep their beautiful light/inner gifts of God to themselves. We all need more confidence in these gifts as God's powerful light within that is given us to shine on others. If we stifle them, they grow weaker; but if we expose and share them, they grow and become stronger.

The Growing Seed and the Sleeping Farmer

4:26 Only Mark has this delightful, humorous, little-known parable. You sow the powerful seed of God's word and then **sleep and rise**. You do absolutely nothing, yet **the earth produces of itself**. In Greek, this expression, "of itself," is *automate*. The comic element becomes stronger when we discover the next activity of Jesus after the crescendo of rising opposition in the last two chapters: it is to take a nice nap for himself on a boat trip (4:38). Sometimes this is the best tactic when difficulties seem overwhelming. Mark may have thought of Psalm 3:5, **I lie down and sleep; I wake again for the Lord sustains me**.

The Tiny Mustard Seed and the Whole World

4:30 The tiny mustard seed can hardly be seen, yet it produces a small tree. This is a striking image of insignificant and perhaps discouraging beginnings but of tremendous far-reaching impact: a tree large enough that the **birds of the air** make nests in it. These birds are a biblical image of the whole world taken from the prophet Daniel (4:10–22)—a world that you will deeply affect by your efforts, small as they may seem.

Jesus Stills a Storm on the Sea of Galilee

4:35 Jesus acts like Elijah, a biblical prophet in intimate communion with the forces of nature. Elijah could pray for a rainstorm and then watch it come (1 Kings 18:41–45); he could also stop rainstorms as well (1 Kings 19:1). However, ancient audiences found a deeper meaning from their scriptural background. In the bible, God appears to be inattentive and sleeping during the storms and trials of life. However an urgent prayer "wakes him up" and he responds with dramatic swift action to calm the storms (Psalm 44:23–26). So after the long series of opposition to Jesus, here is the ultimate "secret weapon" in face of discouragement when it seems that Jesus/God is asleep: to urgently call upon him: **Teacher, do you not care that we are perishing?** The response is immediate: Jesus awakens, takes immediate charge and rebukes the "stormy weather" in our lives so that calm and peace quickly returns.

PATHWAYS TO FURTHER DISCOVERY:

Jesus' parables and stories are really illustrations of his own approach to situations, to people and to God. Look through the gospel for illustrations of this.

PERSONAL JOURNAL SUGGESTION:

Our own life stories can be our best teachers. Each day, look back in your journal a week, a month, six months and a year. Look for patterns of meaning and direction.

The Drowned Pigs and the Healing of the Gerasene Demoniac

5:1 This is one of the most baffling stories for modern readers. Some have even accused Jesus of cruelty to animals because of the two thousand pigs drowned in the sea. Here again, an old key to meaning has been lost. If you saw a sign on a wall,

"Down with the pigs," you would not complain to the SPCA but presume something else is indicated. The gospel story is meant to be a humorous one—a form not immediately apparent to serious, somber readers. The old scriptural key is the biblical story where Pharaoh and his army (the Gentile pigs!) were drowned in the sea while pursuing the people of Israel (Exodus 14). The Jews frequently called the Gentiles, especially the Romans, "pigs." This was because they not only ate that forbidden meat but even regarded pigs as sacred in religious ceremonies.

This story is a counterpart to Jesus' first exorcism in the heart of Judaism, the synagogue. It portrays Jesus' coming victory over the demons controlling the Roman world. Their military might is symbolized by the demons' name, "Legion." The cemetery scene, the unrestrainable, naked, screeching demoniac—these symbolize the powers of death and abusive Roman power that Jesus will overcome. The greatest surprise is that the former "streaker" changes into a calm, clothed man sitting at Jesus' feet in the attitude of a disciple. This sight was so scary and awesome that the people in this Gentile area asked Jesus to leave at this time. He does so, but not before having the transformed demoniac take his place by becoming the first missionary to the Decapolis, ten cities with a largely Gentile population. Once again, God's power shines through most unlikely channels, a source of hope for those in the gospel audience who fear they have little hope to transform the world or even themselves.

Death Turns to Life in the Stories of Two Women

5:21 The cycle of women's stories reaches a climax in what amounts to a double resurrection story. They also continue the death-to-life theme of the previous story. There is also a close connection between the ritual uncleanness in both accounts. The tragedy of the young girl is heart-rending. She has reached the Jewish marriageable age of twelve years and is an only child (implied but made explicit in Luke 8:42). Thus, she was her parents' only hope to continue their name and memory into the future. The other woman also could never marry or have children. In addition, her embarrassing affliction of flowing blood made her perpetually unclean. It was such a powerful ritual taboo that anyone she touched or any article she handled would become unclean as well (Leviticus 15:25–30). We can hardly imagine a more desperate condition than that of this poor social outcast. Even death would have been a kind release for her.

Mark has intertwined these two stories to present them as a teaching example of how to deal with the most impossible situation or human tragedy. We can outline four steps: 1) A profound realization that all human cure seems impossible. The young girl was weak enough to be at the point of death and had already taken her last breath before Jesus arrived. The woman had gone through twelve years of agony and no doctor could help her. 2) Approach to Jesus: the girl through her father, a synagogue leader; the other woman who had heard about Jesus and sneaked up behind him in the crowd, afraid that her contagious uncleanness would lead someone, especially a religious teacher, to shun her. 3) The personal ingredient of total faith and trust: Jesus later said to her, **Daughter, your faith has made you well**. In regard to the young girl, the father does not give up despite a message that his daughter has just died but accepts Jesus' assurance: **Do not fear but only believe**. 4) Personal contact with Jesus: The woman trusted that even touching his cloak would draw out the master's healing power. For the young girl, **He (Jesus) took her by the hand** and even **spoke to her dead spirit**. The author highlights the unusual nature of this cure by noting the exact words that Jesus spoke in his own Aramaic language: **"Talitha cum," which means "Little girl, get up!"**

PATHWAYS TO FURTHER DISCOVERY:

1. Make a list of the women who appear in the gospel. Beside each one, note the part she plays in the total gospel drama.

2. Study the four step sequence in the story of the two women. How is the same sequence found in other gospel cures?

PERSONAL JOURNAL SUGGESTION:

Have a special page where you can note people or situations that need your help and attention. Each day, direct your attention to each one and send energy to each by a short prayer.

Jesus Is Rejected in Nazareth, His Home Town

6:1 It was characteristic of biblical prophets that they often suffered from lack of appreciation from their family, friends and relatives. It always hurts, but this is typical of modern prophets also, such as Gandhi or Martin Luther King. People who know us often consider us quite ordinary and do not always see beyond to our divine source of energy and inspiration. **He (Jesus) could do no deed of power there.** Mark emphasizes the faith of recipients as essential. Jesus is not a magician who wishes to entertain or exhibit special powers.

Jesus Sends Out the Twelve

6:7 Again the typical pattern of apparent failure and retreat followed by new advances. Jesus sends out the twelve to broaden his ministry. They duplicate (as an audience guide) all the things that Jesus did—healings, exorcisms, preaching. At the end, the writer notes, **They healed with oil many who were sick and cured them.** This is a valuable description of how they actually cured: they made a mixture of oil and herbs or used oil alone and rubbed it on affected bodily areas. Christian healers used the same method for many centuries. It is now often called the sacrament of the anointing of the sick.

He ordered them to take nothing for their journey. The only "baggage" will be the powerful message of God (the seed) which only needs good ground. They are to trust that wherever they go they will find some good receptive soil for a miraculous harvest even though there will be rejections and disappointments. This reception will take the form of hospitality and providing for their material needs.

The Martyrdom of John the Baptist

6:14 This story is in such detail because Jesus and the disciples were so deeply touched by the news of their former teacher and colleague. The dark shadow of the cross fell on those who would continue the work of the Baptist. John was a prophet who stood up for moral values at the cost of his own life, and it is the risk that any sincere believer has to take.

Jesus Feeds Five Thousand People

6:30 After hearing the news of the Baptist's death, Jesus said to his disciples, **Come away to a deserted place and let us rest a while**. This time, the sequence of opposition/withdrawal takes on broader dimensions. What will happen to Jesus' presence and work if he meets the same fate as the Baptist? The answer has to do with a new continuing presence of Jesus as a shepherd and leader. The references to **sheep without a shepherd, rest** and **green grass** tell us that the background of Psalm 23, **The Lord is my shepherd**, is present. Jesus will remain with them as a nourishing shepherd. Mark will bring this out through the loaves' multiplication stories.

Once again, a modern audience may miss a great deal without the background of the Hebrew scriptures. There we find the theme that God multiplies bread when it is shared with others at his command. For example, a poor widow and her son shared their last bit of flour and bread with the prophet Elijah. As a result, God promised that her flour would mysteriously replenish itself as long as necessary (1 Kings 17:8–16). Also, the prophet Elisha at God's command fed a hundred men with only twenty small pancake-shaped loaves (2 Kings 4:42–44). As a result, they ate and were completely satisfied as the bread mysteriously multiplied. When God gave the people of Israel bread in the desert, there was always enough for everyone. This happened because, at the day's end, there was a "miracle" of sharing as those present equally divided all the bread they had gathered (Exodus 16:16–18).

In view of the above background, when the disciples came to Jesus to present the needs of the hungry crowd, Jesus gave them the impossible command, **You give them something to eat**. When the disciples naturally objected, he asked, **How many loaves have you? Go and see**. After inquiring around the crowds, they find a few people willing to share the very limited amount of bread they carried for their journey, a meager five loaves and two fishes. **Taking the five loaves and the two**

fish...he blessed and broke the loaves and gave them to his disciples to set before the crowd. (These words are remarkably similar to those used by Jesus at the last supper, to which they are an important link.) Jesus mysteriously continues sharing the bread until five thousand people are completely satisfied. It appears to be a *new bread* since twelve baskets are left over from only five loaves to start with. Just as the last supper can only be understood in light of Jesus' death, so also the feeding narrative needs the following episode.

Jesus Walks on Water

6:45 At night Jesus remained behind to pray on the mountain while the disciples crossed the sea of Galilee in a boat ahead of him. The disciples have an unusual night vision of Jesus walking on the water as they struggle against a storm. Even today, the expression "to walk on water" means to accomplish the impossible. In those days, it meant to overcome the powers of death, just as the Israelite people did when they crossed the Red Sea. The sequence of events—sharing bread, going out to pray, overcoming death and returning to the disciples—foreshadow Jesus' last supper, prayer at Gethsemane, death and resurrection. Only then will the audience understand the meaning of Jesus' bread. That is why Mark ends with the observation, **They did not understand about the loaves.**

PATHWAYS TO FURTHER DISCOVERY:

According to Jewish custom, when Jesus took bread, he blessed (pronounced a blessing). Even today, orthodox Jews do not eat, drink or perform special other actions without a formula of blessing. For example, the blessing for bread used today and for many centuries is, "Blessed be thou, O Lord, Our God, King of the Universe, who brings forth bread from the earth." This is an acknowledgement that beneath bread is God the source of all life and nourishment. Find out more about this custom of Jesus and Jews to use blessings to find God's presence in what seems most ordinary and commonplace. What effect does the habit of "blessings" have on life?

PERSONAL JOURNAL SUGGESTION:

In the evening, look back on each day with a sense of wonder and acknowledgement (blessing) for God's presence even in the most ordinary things and events in life. Check on the progress you are making each day in having more "full stops" through at least the inner habit of blessing.

Healing the Sick in Gennesaret

6:53 This is a transition story broadening Jesus' apostolate and preparing for a second multiplication of loaves that will extend to the whole world.

Jesus Breaks the Barriers to Table Fellowship

7:1 However, a formidable obstacle blocks the way toward one bread and one world. According to custom and tradition, Jewish people had to purify their hands from Gentile dust before eating. Food had to be pure and cooked by their own hands, not foreigners'. Also, they could not eat certain foods, especially pork, which were considered unclean in the bible. These biblically derived requirements made any real association and table fellowship with Gentiles practically impossible. Was there any authoritative word from Jesus to deal with this most difficult impediment? There was no specific word, since Jesus himself kept all these customs and rarely came into contact with Gentiles. However, he did give a principle on one occasion that could be a guide: **There is nothing outside a person that by going in can defile, but the things that come out are what defile**. From this statement Mark made the conclusion for his audience: **(Thus he declared all foods clean)**.

A Foreign Woman Opens Up a Path to the Whole World

7:24 Here another anonymous woman, representing the non-Jewish world, initiates a marvelous new direction in salvation history. Jesus is staying in mostly Gentile territory in southern Lebanon, but only privately. So when a Gentile woman asks for her daughter's cure, he responds, **Let the children be fed first**. Jesus said this because the scriptures had spoken of the coming messiah as being first of all for the Jewish people, and the Gentiles only joining them at the end of time. This was the message in the vision of the great prophet Isaiah (2:2). This woman, however, will not take "no" for an answer. She persistently asks with deep faith to share this bread, even if only crumbs from the messianic banquet—the feeding that has just taken place. Jesus is deeply moved by her faith and replies in two ways: first, by curing her daughter from a distance—the only time in this gospel. For the Gentile gospel audience this is exciting; it means that Jesus heals them also across distance and time. Second, Jesus himself begins a second multiplication of bread that will answer the desire of the whole world that this woman represents.

A Deaf Man Hears Jesus' Voice

7:31 The theme of universality with its joy and excitement continues for the largely Gentile audience (which we are!). In the same Gentile territory, Jesus heals a man who cannot hear or speak. The crowds remark, **He has done everything well**. This is a refrain from the great universal creation theme in Genesis 1. There, at the end of each day, God saw that everything he had created was good. Like the healed man, the audience also can hear what they have never heard before and speak as never before in God's new creation.

Jesus Feeds Four Thousand People

8:1 Many details in this story show that it symbolizes a feeding of the non-Jewish world. For example, it takes place on Jesus' initiative in typical Gentile territory; the people come **from a great distance**; the numbers: **seven**, the number of fullness in regard to the original loaves and the baskets left over; **four**, the universal number of north, south, east, west. Contrast this to the typically Jewish numbers of the first feeding which are "five," representing the first five books of the bible, and "twelve," representing the twelve tribes of Israel. And most interesting is the phrase **After giving thanks** where the Greek root *eucharistia* is used instead of the more Jewish "blessing" in the first story.

The Yeast of the Pharisees and Herod
in Contrast to the Mystery of One Bread for One World

8:11 A rude awakening and contrast comes on Jesus' return to Israel when Pharisees ask for a sign from heaven instead of the interior faith we have seen in the Greek woman. The sign they asked would be some great external and cosmic event such as thunder, lightning, or an earthquake. Jesus refuses. The only sign he promotes is the humble one of faith that there can be a new food language for the world.

Jesus has to warn his disciples not to fall into the same trap as their opponents: **Beware of the yeast of the Pharisees and the yeast of Herod.** Like them, the disciples also have trouble with Jesus' simple sign of bread taken and shared at his command. The key words are the **one loaf** they have in the boat. It should have been a reminder of what Jesus wanted to do: to unite the world by sharing the same one bread. So Jesus challenges them and the gospel audience to open their eyes and ears to this new meaning. They need to **remember** this whenever they think of eating food. Whenever they **remember**, they will experience that the person of Jesus is behind a new bread destined to bring the world together.

The Healing of the Blind Man and the Gospel Transition Point

8:22 This story marks a transition point in Mark's dramatic narrative. We have just read that the disciples were blind to the full meaning of the loaves. But there is hope for them and disciples of any time. Jesus can open their eyes to understand who he is and what is the mysterious bread that he gives. This will take place in the two steps symbolized by the cure of the blind man. The first step will be the partial opening of Peter's eyes in the next scene; the second will be Jesus' coming instruction on the Son of Man and the way of the cross.

PATHWAYS TO FURTHER DISCOVERY:

Trace the importance of bread/food as it appears in the gospel. As you do so, put together the ingredients of Jesus' new food language.

PERSONAL JOURNAL SUGGESTION:

In the biblical tradition, bread shared at God's command multiplies in a mysterious manner. Each week, try to put aside a meal or snacks and use the savings for the needy and hungry. In your journal, note how this "fasting that others may feast" affects you and others. If you wish to join many others with the same idea, write "Skip-A-Meal," Santa Clara University, Santa Clara, CA 95053 for further information.

Peter Confesses His Faith in Jesus as Messiah

8:27 The first gradual opening of eyes (from 8:24) takes place as Peter makes his confession of faith: **You are the messiah**. But Jesus silences him because it is insufficient and can be misunderstood by people looking for a military messiah or a powerful Jesus returning from heaven to conquer their enemies. At this point, we begin the second stage of eye-opening with the startling words: **Then he began to teach them that the Son of Man must undergo great suffering...be rejected...killed...and after three days rise again**. Mark will have three such predictions (here, 9:30 and 10:32), each followed by an instruction on how to follow Jesus' way.

The title **Son of Man** again reminds the audience of the prophet Daniel in chapter 7. There, the title goes beyond that of coming judge to represent the people of God in their sufferings, humiliation and exaltation. The strong word **must** shows a necessity in God's plan as found in the scriptures. This way of God is difficult so we sympathize with Peter as he complains about it to Jesus. Jesus sharply replies, **Get behind me, Satan**, for Peter is tempting him to abandon God's plan.

8:34 Then Jesus begins the first section of teachings on discipleship by saying to the gospel audience: **If any want to become my followers, let them deny themselves, and take**

up their cross and follow me. If anyone is ashamed to follow this way, then the Son of Man in his return as judge will likewise be ashamed of that person. Here we note for the first time the coming of the Son of Man as future judge. Mark expected this within the lifetime of the first gospel audience, so he notes Jesus' words that some present will not die **until they see that the kingdom of God has come with power**.

The Transfiguration of Jesus

9:2 To confirm Jesus' teaching on the return of the Son of Man and the cross, Mark gives us a preview or "coming attractions" of that return in the transfiguration story. The **high mountain** recalls the mountain where **Moses** met God and his face was **transfigured** with divine light (Exodus 34:29–35). Jesus will return like **Elijah** whom God took up into heaven in a fiery chariot to await his command to return to earth in the new age (2 Kings 2:11–12; Malachi 4:5). The focal point of the vision is God's thunderous voice like that on Mount Sinai: **This is my Son, my beloved; listen to him**. At Jesus' baptism, God spoke directly and secretly to him and he faithfully obeyed. Now we are the audience as the divine voice tells us to really listen to (obey) the very difficult words of Jesus about taking up the cross and following him even at great personal risk.

The Coming of Elijah

9:4 Jesus cautions them to tell no one about the glorious vision because it would draw attention to his powers and distract from the way of the cross. The disciples' question represents an audience concern: What about the return of Elijah promised in the scriptures (Malachi 4:5)? The answer is that Elijah has indeed returned in the person of John the Baptist in view of his courageous prophetic suffering and death at Herod's hands (6:17–29). In this way he has prepared the way for Jesus' own suffering and return.

The Healing of the Possessed Boy

9:14 This story, like the transfiguration, strengthens the audience to follow the difficult way of Jesus. The desperate case is a boy with frightful seizures that made him speechless and reduced him to a deathlike stupor. The boy's father had brought him to some disciples for a cure but they were unable to help. The desperate father then introduced him to Jesus with the words, **If you are able to do anything, have pity on us and help us**. His idea is that Jesus would have superior powers to those of his disciples. However, in a striking manner, Jesus turns his words around: **If you are able**—placing the brunt on the faith of the recipient—**all things are possible for the one who believes**.

The man humbly replies that he does not have that kind of faith and asks for it as a gift. This is a great relief for the audience. They also can be doubtful, wavering and even argue with God. They identify with the disciples' question, **Why couldn't we cast it out?** The answer sounds simple—**prayer**. However, this does not just mean repeating a formula. It means total, intensive, persevering prayer that requires an inner struggle like that of the boy's father.

PATHWAYS TO FURTHER DISCOVERY:

Study the sequence of references to faith in Mark. What are the qualities of this faith that emerge in the gospel stories?

PERSONAL JOURNAL SUGGESTION:

Often we feel the need of complaining to someone. The sign of a good friend is the ability to really listen and understand in a non-judgmental way. This is an essential part of a relationship. When you visit sick persons, encourage them to express their feelings. A journal time is often a good opportunity to dialogue with God as a good friend. Sometimes we will just feel like complaining, as Job did in the bible. God encourages you to do so; sometimes this is the best prayer, for it is truth, and truth makes us like God.

Jesus Foretells a Second Time
His Death and Resurrection

9:30 The repeated reference to lack of understanding (9:32) is puzzling unless we remember that Mark considers the understanding of the cross as an ongoing process for the audience. The central theme of this second section on discipleship is that of the **child**, with stories of children told directly or indirectly.

Who Is the Greatest?

9:33 Jesus' disciples were as competitive as we are today (hard to believe!). Jesus' approach is not a negative, "Don't argue or compete," but actually an encouragement to compete even more strongly for the "lowest" position of service: **Whoever wishes to be the first must be last and servant of all.** Jesus places **a little child** in their midst as an object lesson. **Whoever welcomes one such child welcomes me.** It is not a matter of what we do but how we do it. A welcome for a child, on the bottom power rung of society, is a welcome to Jesus and the God who sent him.

Jesus' View on Competition from Outsiders

9:38 No less a VIP than John tries to stop an outsider, a Jewish exorcist who was not a follower of Jesus. Jesus extends the example of welcome to an outsider who is like the "little one" or child above. Mark's gospel warns against exclusivism. Again it is the quality of the reception that matters—even a **cup of water to drink** counts as given to the messiah and merits a special reward.

Abuse and Temptation of Little Ones

9:42 The theme of children and little ones continues with a severe warning to those who would lead them into sin or abuse them. Children are a distinct priority in Jesus' teaching. The words **hell** and **Gehenna** (as the textual note points out) refer to the continually smoking garbage dump in the valley of Gehenna outside Jerusalem. It is a symbol of God's special warning and judgment for those who hurt his precious children.

Jesus' Teaching on Divorce

10:1 The theme of the little ones extends to their mothers who have often been victims of discriminatory, male-dominated civil and even religious legislation. According to the biblical regulations in Deuteronomy 24:4, men could dismiss their wives by a written notice of dismissal, as if dealing with property (this was usually true of Roman legislation as well). Ordinarily, wives could not do the same. Jesus pushes back the basis of marriage to the creation story in Genesis 2:24. There it is a personal covenant between two people, rather than a matter of property legislation.

Can such a covenant ever be broken? Mark has no specific answer. However the gospel presumes that God's covenant with us has priority over any human covenant. Even the marriage covenant at times must yield to the priorities of the kingdom of God. The apostle Paul dealt with a particular example of this in 1 Corinthians 7:12–16. It is interesting that Mark, unlike Matthew (6:32; 19:9), expands Jesus' words to apply to a woman divorcing her husband, a situation more common in the Greek world than in the Jewish world. Jesus' teaching on divorce, if taken in context, is not legislative and restrictive, but liberating. The influence of many western legalistic interpreters through the centuries has changed the context and atmosphere of Jesus' marriage instruction.

Jesus' Special Blessing for Children Then and Now

10:13 This is a doublet of 9:33–37 for special emphasis and literary enclosure. The attention, affection, and blessing of children by the master, despite the protests of busy, stern disciples, show where the priorities of time should be in the kingdom. Jesus **blessed** the children. In the bible, a blessing is a special communication of God's energy. It is sometimes an indication of succession, as when Jacob blessed his children before dying. Children in spirit are the real inner successors of

Jesus in contrast to the disciples competing for distinctions in 9:34.

Jesus' Teachings About Money and Real Wealth

10:17 Perhaps contrasting with the children's blessing above, here is the story of a man who considered himself blessed by God in his many possessions. He had sincerely kept God's commandments since a youth and asked Jesus if there was anything else he could do. **Jesus, looking at him, loved him.** This represents the loving invitation of grace going out to a gospel audience. However, discipleship is not easy: **Go, sell what you own, and give the money to the poor, and you will have treasure in heaven; then come, follow me.** To follow Jesus calls for a lifelong priority for the needs of the hungry and poor. This choice, then and now, is very difficult. **When the rich man heard this, he was shocked and went away grieving, for he had many possessions.** Jesus follows here the biblical teaching on land and property: it belongs to God, is lent for our use and is meant to be equitably shared by all. The sadness and grieving of this man in facing this prospect was simply too much for him. He is anonymous because he represents many in the gospel audience.

Since Jesus' teaching on money is so difficult, he repeats it three times, finally through a vivid and humorous image: **It is easier for a camel to go through the eye of a needle than for someone who is rich to enter the kingdom of God.** The apostles, like the rich man, were astounded in view of the common feeling that rich people were blessed by God. They said to one another, **Who then can be saved?** Jesus replies that the ability to share generously is God's gift and very contrary to the human tendency toward selfishness: **For mortals it is impossible, but for God all things are possible.**

From what follows, we learn that Jesus' focus is not just on giving up, but on finding unexpected additional personal wealth through sharing. Jesus said to Peter that the temporary loss of individual wealth would result in a new common wealth in communities that truly share. This common wealth, unlike earthly riches, cannot be taken away but endures into the next life. God's way is the reversal of ordinary human priorities: **But many who are first will be last and the last will become first.**

PATHWAYS TO FURTHER DISCOVERY:

Trace Jesus' "upside-down" theology (11:31) through the gospel and compare it to ordinary views in the world.

PERSONAL JOURNAL SUGGESTION:

As we grow older we often suppress the child within. Look back to what you most enjoyed and found meaningful when young/a child. See what you can regain and experience fruitfully in your present life.

The Third Prediction of Jesus' Death and Resurrection

10:32 Jerusalem, the capital city, is now the immediate focus of the third prediction. As a prophet, Jesus must be ready to preach there and meet his most powerful opposition at the center of religious and political authority. Accordingly, there is an atmosphere of foreboding and fear as Jesus walks ahead of his disciples on the Jerusalem road. Jesus' predictions become more explicit and ominous.

The Special Request of James and John for Favored Status

10:35 James and John were among the special leaders of the twelve. Yet even they were looking for special niches of power at Jesus' side in the capital city. Jesus warns them that they do not know what they are asking for. To be at Jesus' **right hand or left hand** (the audience will later hear) is the place of those crucified with Jesus on Calvary (15:27). To be truly at his side, they would need to be **baptized** (plunged into) his death and share his **cup** of suffering. Jesus does not grant prizes in his kingdom. The story surprises us because we imagine Jesus' first followers with halos around their heads and tend to imagine that competition and desire for power had no place among them. Mark believes in honesty and tells the story because he knows from experience that these realities of human weakness have plagued the church at all times and need to brought out in the open.

10:41 When the ten heard this, they began to be angry with James and John. The other ten disciples seem to have caught the same "capital fever" as they approach Jerusalem. Mark was well aware of abusive Roman authority as he wrote Jesus' words, **Among the Gentiles, those whom they recognize as their rulers lord it over them.** Yet the evangelist was even more sensitive to abusive church/community authority through Jesus' words addressed directly to the audience: **It is not so among you.** Jesus' followers are to be remarkable for loving service of others, not control over them. The supreme example is that of the Son of Man, who though coming as judge in power **came not to be served but to serve and to give his life as a ransom for many.** The final words are adapted from the image of the servant of the Lord in Isaiah 53 who offered his life to God as if a temple sacrifice.

The Healing of the Blind Bartimaeus and Its Symbolism

10:46 Jericho, near the Dead Sea, marks the beginning of Jesus' final ascent to Jerusalem. This healing is very meaningful for an audience desiring in spirit to accompany Jesus to Jerusalem. As part of the audience, we are blind to the meaning of what will happen to Jesus in Jerusalem and what it means to follow him there. The shouting, urgent prayer of Bartimaeus becomes that of anyone in the audience, **My teacher, let me see again.** Once our sight is restored, like Bartimaeus we can **follow him on the way.**

Jesus' Triumphal Entry into Jerusalem

11:1 The ancient kings of Israel had entered the capital in grandiose military style. The messianic entry of Jesus is a deliberately planned sharp contrast. He humbly enters the city seated on a donkey with a few disciples and followers. It resembled a clown act to teach his outlook on pretense and grandeur. As Mark's audience studied the scriptures, the inner Spirit of Jesus helped them understand the story in terms of Zechariah 9:9, **Your king will come to you, triumphant and victorious is he, humble and riding on a donkey.** The text describes a messiah of peace who will destroy the chariots and weapons of war. Mark tells the story so the listeners can replay it often in imagination and liturgical drama, singing with the crowds, **Hosanna! Blessed is the one who comes in the name of the Lord**.

Jesus Curses a Fig Tree

11:12 Should ecologists be disturbed? Not if they have a sense of humor and realize it was another trick of the master to make them understand the meaning of the temple cleansing. The fig tree is a well-known symbol of the people of God. Jesus, as a prophet, is hungry and seeks fruit from them. A curse in the scriptures indicates responsibility for rejecting God's voice in a prophet.

Jesus Cleanses the Temple

11:15 There is no question of wrongdoing in those who were buying and selling or changing money in the vast outside temple court. Jews came to the feasts from all over the world and needed to change their money into local currency. Then they would buy the required animals for sacrifice offered for sale in the same temple area. Jesus' symbolic cleansing of the temple area focused on the priority of prayer in a new temple designed for all the world's peoples. These Gentiles had been excluded by a formidable wall around part of the temple area that warned them to go no further under penalty of death.

The central point of the story lies in Jesus' words, **My house shall be called a house of prayer for all the nations**. Mark draws attention to the chief priests' and scribes' reaction to those words. We can hardly imagine their shock at the very thought that the sacred temple (under their supervision!) would be a place where uncircumcised and pork-eating Gentiles would gather to pray with them. **When…they heard it, they kept looking for a way to kill him**. In contrast, **the whole crowd was spellbound by his teaching**. This could well describe the gospel audience. As they listened to the story they knew that the temple had already been destroyed. Yet

God had turned tragedy into triumph by giving them Jesus as a new spiritual temple of worship, a house of prayer for the whole world. In this form of worship, the buying and selling of animals, as symbolically stopped by Jesus, was no longer needed.

The Surprising Lesson of the Fig Tree

11:20 To understand the humor in this story, we need the comic background of the book of Jonah. The author pictures God as shriveling up a tree in a day as an object lesson for Jonah. That Hebrew prophet was angered that God had not destroyed the Gentiles of Nineveh according to his threat, and he was still waiting for it to happen (4:6). God gave him a shade tree as Jonah watched in the hot sun. The next morning (as after the temple story) Jonah found that the tree had withered up, leaving him to roast in the sun. The prophet was angry enough to want to die. God scolded him for being more concerned about the tree for his shade than over hundreds of thousands of Gentiles saved from destruction.

With the above comic background, we see that the "dense" Peter like Jonah is more concerned (like some people today!) about the fig tree than about the impact of Jesus' revolutionary announcement about creating a new world temple where no one is excluded. It all sounds so impossible that Jesus continues with another humorous illustration—that of getting a mountain moved into the sea. Jesus explains the secret about how this can be done: **If you do not doubt, but believe that what you say will come to pass, it will be done for you**. The recipe for success is having a faith so strong that you imagine the result even before you ask for it: **Whatever you ask for in prayer, believe that you have received it already and it will be yours**. An open, pure heart is needed for this kind of faith, so Mark adds a special quality of this prayer, similar to the Lord's prayer found only in Matthew and Luke: We should stand up to pray only after forgiving others so we may be open to God's gifts and forgiveness.

The Question of Jesus' Authority

11:27 Authority questions dominate Jesus' encounters in the capital city, the center of religious and political authority. Here we see that Jesus' authority becomes a burning issue for the chief priests, scribes and elders. This story shows that Jesus' authority comes from the prophetic voice of God, which was behind John the Baptist and, we might add, any other prophet past or modern. This is always above institutional religious authorities who must always answer to it.

The Parable of the Ungrateful Tenants of the Vineyard

12:1 The theme of prophetic activity and authority continues. The introduction and end of the parable show that it is directed against **them**, the institutional leaders. **A vineyard** is a familiar scriptural image of God's people. The parable is not directed against the people, but the **tenants**, their leaders, who are supposed to care for the vineyard. The parable's theme is God's care for his people, sending prophet after prophet to their leaders and yet meeting increasing rejection and even physical abuse. (We notice the superiority of the prophetic voice over the institutional voice.) The parable is really true to history: Jeremiah, who also prophesied the temple's destruction, was arrested, scourged and finally put to death; Isaiah also suffered much and was finally executed (according to tradition). Yet God's love is not frustrated. He finally sends even his Son, who is seized and put to death. Once again, God's response is not to give up but to expand his care and give his vineyard to be tended by other leaders in place of the former tenants. The formerly rejected ones, the outsiders, become part of a new and greater building of God—another echo of the temple story. Mark's audience rejoices at their inclusion in the parable but is reminded that the prophetic voice of God ever calls for renewal; complacency will result in their places being taken by others.

Should Taxes Be Paid to Rome?

12:13 Many revolutions have started with a refusal to pay taxes—as with the Boston tea party. The question to Jesus is loaded with danger. To say "yes" is to betray the freedom aspirations of people; to say "no" labels Jesus and his followers of any time as dangerous revolutionaries. Jesus' answer is literally, **Give to Caesar the things that are Caesar's and to God the things that are God's**. This answer has been famous through history, but sometimes not understood in its context. To "give to God what is God's" means total service to God at every moment of life as enjoined by the first and second commandments. Thus, "To give to Caesar" can be permissible only if it takes nothing away from total service of God. As the gospel audience we are **utterly amazed**, for authorities often invoke God's name and try to make us believe they are God's voice. However, we may only obey them and their laws when they serve God's causes (see Romans 13:1–7).

Does Scripture Teach That the Resurrection Is for All People?

12:18 Most Jews in Jesus' time believed in the ultimate resurrection of the faithful dead. They based their belief mainly on the books of Daniel (e.g. chapter 12) and 1 and 2 Maccabees. However, the Sadducees were a group of prominent Jews who only followed the teachings of the ancient Torah, the first five books of the bible. Those books contain no definite teaching about the resurrection. The humorous story about the woman with seven husbands is actually based on the biblical levirate law in Deuteronomy 25:5–10. This is still observed today by many Jewish people, at least technically. Jesus answers first that the resurrection does not carry on inferior–superior levels of gender distinction ("those who marry" are men and "those given in marriage" are women). Secondly, Jesus bases the resurrection on God's revelation to Moses in the burning bush— a symbol of continual life and energy (Exodus 3:1–6). The God of our ancestors, Abraham and Sarah, Isaac and Rebecca, Jacob and his wives, is a God who is the source of all life. A relationship to Life itself can never be broken.

What Is the One Most Important Commandment?

12:28 The scribe's question, much disputed for thousands of years, was **Which commandment is first of all?** Everyone wants to know what is the most important thing that life or God requires of us. Jesus replies in the words of the favorite Jewish prayer over the centuries, a prayer that was memorized and recited over and over again during the day and especially at the hour of death. Those words express a beautiful totality of devotion—mind, heart and feelings—so there is really no place for what is more or less important. But Jesus continues on the same level, **The second is this, "You shall love your neighbor as yourself."** The scribe realizes the radical conclusion that loving one's neighbor is far superior to all the temple offerings, buildings and religious rites. This is another temple reference especially important for Mark's audience in the first centuries when they had no temples or church buildings but met in private homes.

The Mysterious Nature of the Messiah as Son of David

12:35 This puzzling passage is important for the insight it gives on how the early church interpreted scripture. They consider it inspired by God: **David by the Holy Spirit said.** With this view, the Holy Spirit, the author of scripture, could bring to believers a fullness of meaning even beyond the authors' scope. In this story that fullness of meaning implies a very exalted image of the messiah as seated at the right hand of God, a phrase taken into early creeds and still used today.

Jesus' Conclusion to the Jerusalem Dialogues

12:38 This is a brief conclusion to Jesus' dialogues with the Jerusalem authorities—there will be no more in this gospel. Like much Jewish literature, Jesus warns against pretentious religion teachers. The audience might smile at the familiar picture of religious leaders in fancy robes, prizing distinguished titles and sitting in specially reserved seats. The mention of **widows** is a connecting link and contrast to the next story of the **poor widow** that will be an introduction to Jesus' last will and testament in the next chapter.

PATHWAYS TO FURTHER DISCOVERY:

The Temple was supremely important to the Gospel audience as the special place of God's presence. Look through the references to the Temple in the last five chapters of Mark. In what way does Mark present Jesus as assuming the role and function of the Temple?

PERSONAL JOURNAL SUGGESTION:

Try Mark's secret of "infallible" prayer (11:23–24) in the following way: 1) Vividly imagine what you would really like to have or be in your life. 2) Picture it as if it had already taken place. 3) Pray fervently for God's help in making it come to pass. Recommended dosage: once a day. This is the "prayer that moves mountains."

The Offering of the Poor Widow

12:41 In striking contrast to the last incident, this story is a beautiful introduction to Jesus' last will and testament in chapter 13. **The poor widow,** unlike the scribes and rich people, did not just leave a donation in the temple treasury, she **put in everything she had, all she had to live on**. Thus she is a living example of what Jesus will ask for in his coming last discourse: disciples willing to give everything, even life itself, for what they believe in.

Jesus Foretells the Temple's Destruction and His Return

13:1 Chapter 13 is crucial for understanding Mark's gospel. Jesus' last discourse and final testament informs his disciples what the future holds for them. By the time this gospel was written, the temple had already been destroyed in the recent past. This was a great shock both to Christians and Jews alike. It had been their religious center and place of worship as God's dwelling place. Some Christian prophets were teaching that the temple's destruction was a divine sign heralding the imminent end of the world. During this time, Jesus would return in power to liberate them from their Roman oppressors and start a new age. Those prophets pointed to many signs to support their predictions. Mark regards their teachings as false and dangerous.

The scene takes place on Mount Olivet, facing the Jerusalem temple, a traditional place for God's coming judgment. Jesus predicts that the temple will be destroyed. This was like Jeremiah who had prophesied that the first temple would be destroyed by the Babylonians in 587 B.C. Jesus warns his disciples about Christian prophets who announce this, using the typical prophetic first person in Jesus' name, "I am he."

When you hear of wars and rumors of wars, do not be alarmed. Some of those false teachers claimed that God's final battle against the forces of evil was about to begin. Jewish literature had predicted such a final conflict. It is interesting that government and military leaders through the centuries have always tried to make their soldiers believe they are fighting for both God and country in a great struggle against evil. Thus soldiers could feel that even if they lost their lives they would become heroic and glorious martyrs. The false prophets also made predictions of natural phenomena such as earthquakes to bolster their claims. (Much publicity often goes with such predictions, but very little news about their failure.)

From these false signs, Jesus turns to the true ones which will occur in the disciples' lives. Their future fate will be no different from that of Jesus; this will be the only real sign. Like Jesus, they will be handed over to **councils, synagogues and kings**. This will not be a disaster but an opportunity for witness: **a testimony (martyrion) to them**. This will be the only way to win over others (like the way Jesus will win over a hardened centurion at his crucifixion).

13:10 **And the good news (gospel) must first be proclaimed to all the nations.** This preaching to the world is another necessary prelude to Jesus' return. However, it will only be possible by the above suffering witness of disciples. In this way they will have an active part in bringing about Jesus' return. Consequently, believers need not fear for the future, for their work is that of the Holy Spirit. This Spirit will speak through them even though the most shocking things happen such as betrayal by family members and friends. Disciples can be confident in Jesus' words, **The one who endures to the end will be saved**.

The Lesson of the Temple's Destruction

13:14 Therefore, the tragic and sacrilegious destruction of the temple does not mean that God will swiftly intervene to destroy their enemies. Christians must not follow military or government leaders who proclaim this. Instead, Jesus advises flight: **those in Judea must flee to the mountains.** *As messiah of peace, Jesus does not support those who proclaim holy wars against evildoers.* They should choose to flee rather than hope God will give them a victory over Rome despite overwhelming odds against them.

Again Jesus warns, three times in all, against false messiahs and false prophets who **produce signs and omens to lead astray if possible even the elect.** Their teaching seduces many people because no one wants to be a loser and surely God Almighty is on the winning side. It explains why Jesus and many prophets past and present receive such a limited popular reception. Prophets of peace and non-violence rarely gain a majority support in their lifetimes. After their death, however, guilt often prompts people to name streets after them and declare holidays in their name.

The Final Return of the Son of Man to the Whole World

13:24 The above fulfilled prediction of the temple gives the audience additional confirmation that Jesus' further prediction of his return will also be accomplished. However, this return will not be local or connected with the temple's tragic destruction. Instead, it will be a manifestation to the whole world. The sun, moon and stars in the text stand for all creation. The Son of Man **will send his angels to gather his elect from the four winds.** Thus, there will be *no judgment* for any of the gospel listeners who are not ashamed to stand up for what they believe (8:38).

The Need for Watchful Waiting and Prayer

13:32 **But about that day or hour no one knows.** This is a clear answer to the disciples' question about the time of Jesus' return. Yet despite its clarity, hundreds of self-proclaimed prophets through the ages have deluded people into believing that they have secret revelations about the exact time of the world's end and Jesus' return. In recent years the most tragic has been the David Koresh sect in Waco, Texas.

Yet despite this, Christianity does look forward to the future with hope combined with a present sense of responsibility. Since we have no knowledge or control over the future, Jesus repeatedly warns us to be **alert** and not **asleep** lest we miss once-and-for-all opportunities. This is illustrated in the concluding parable: **It is like a man going on a journey, when he leaves home and puts his servants in charge all with their own work**. Jesus is like that man on a journey, with each of us having our work or charge. We are asked to be faithful to the talent the master has given us any time when he asks for an accounting.

PATHWAYS TO FURTHER DISCOVERY:

Jesus' last will describes a conflict with evil in the world. In our own times, the struggle escalates in intensity regarding crime, violence and wars. How would Jesus' way as described in chapter 13 compare or contrast with other ways of combating evil that you have heard about?

PERSONAL JOURNAL SUGGESTION:

To win a battle against evil forces outside of us, we must first win our own personal battles against forces dictating how we should act. These are often called "addictions." How can they be detected? One test is to be aware of the things I feel compelled to do despite better judgment. Note in your journal examples of this and your efforts to overcome them.

The Plot To Kill Jesus and the Bethany Anointing

14:1 The heart of the gospel, the passion narrative, now begins as the Jerusalem leaders seek to arrest Jesus secretly and execute him. Just as the poor widow's story introduced and exemplified Jesus' last testament, so also the Bethany woman introduces the story of Jesus' last days. She is purposely anonymous to give hope to all the anonymous and unhistorical persons among believers who wonder if their lives can be really worthwhile.

Women often performed the welcoming ritual of hospitality by anointing a guest's head with oil. But this lady's ointment is extravagant and lavish—she had worked hard for a year or more to earn the money to buy it. The breaking of the jar (like similar such broken jars found in ancient cemeteries) symbolized the *pouring out* of her life. This imitates Jesus, for the same word describes his blood at the last supper (14:25). The fragrant perfumed ointment, *nard*, found only in the biblical love poems of the Song of Solomon, symbolizes the deep affection in her heart. Some disciples were angry about this and scolded the woman for her wastefulness: Would not a large donation to the poor be a better way to honor Jesus?

The above contrast is similar to the widow's story where the woman's gift of herself outweighed all the rich donations to the temple treasury. Jesus replies by stressing the personal nature of the Bethany woman's gift: **Why do you trouble her? She has performed a good service for me. For you always have the poor with you…but you will not always have me**. It is always possible to help the poor but the total personal and affectionate gift of the woman is truly unique. She has appreciated the meaning of Jesus' coming death. Her anointing symbolizes that he will be the messiah ("anointed one") through the offering of his life: **She has anointed my body beforehand for its burial**. Parallel to the ending of the widow's story (12:43), Jesus concludes with a solemn **Amen I say to you** statement (this is the literal form of "Truly I say to you"): **Wherever the good news is proclaimed in the whole world, what she has done will be told in remembrance of her**. Following this woman's leadership, the personal devotion and service of seemingly unknown and anonymous people will make possible the spread of the gospel to the whole world.

The Betrayal of Judas

14:10 In contrast, Judas must have been among those who scolded the Bethany woman. At least the gospel of John thought so (12:4). Over the centuries, Judas' character has become progressively blackened, yet we have little information about his inner motives. One possibility is that he simply did his duty to the puppet government and denounced Jesus as a potential and therefore dangerous messiah. For the audience he represents those who play it safe and are not willing to take the risks necessary to follow Jesus.

The Passover Meal with Jesus' Disciples

14:12 **On the first day of the feast of Unleavened Bread when the Passover lamb is sacrificed.** Mark explains the meaning of Jesus' action through its strong parallel to the Passover ritual. The ritual of the Passover meal was enacted according to God's precise instructions (Exodus 12). This gave the ritual its power. In parallel, Jesus gives exact orders about the planning of this meal. There are unusual circumstances such as the meeting of a man carrying a water jar who brings them to a furnished banquet hall. This shows that the divine plan is beneath what is happening on the surface. The meal will indeed be **the Lord's supper**, arranged at his command and therefore having his power.

Evening sundown signaled the time for the Passover meal to begin and Jesus arrived with his disciples. Unfortunately, art masterpieces showing only Jesus and twelve male disciples have given us a wrong image. Women had to be present according to the passover regulations of Exodus 12. As they were eating, Jesus made the shocking announcement that one of his table companions would betray him. He assures them that this is not just a horrible accident but that God's plan will work despite it and even through it.

The Institution of the Lord's Supper

14:22 The loaves' multiplication has already prepared for this: the disciples are to remember Jesus when they break bread (8:18). Now the evangelist presents the ritual way to do this as it was planned and executed by Jesus. The loaves' multiplication illustrated the nourishing quality of bread given by Jesus as good shepherd. But there is also another central bread meaning, that of covenant or contract. Meals in ancient times often sealed contracts and agreements between people. The English language has a relic of this in the word "companion," from the Latin roots "cum" (with) and "panis" (bread).

Also, bread has a strong identification motif: "We are what we eat." This motif is especially strong when the host furnishes the bread and serves it by hand. Thus the command, **Take, this is my body**, is an offer to be truly identified with Jesus as a disciple. The shared **cup** strengthens this and brings out the covenant aspect. For example, at a Jewish wedding, even to this day, bride and bridegroom drink from the same cup to signify their covenant with one another. **So all of them drank from it.**

The words, **This is my blood**, recall Moses' words when he sealed a covenant between God and his people on Mount Sinai. Moses took sacrificial blood and sprinkled it on the people, saying, **See the blood of the covenant that the LORD has made with you** (Exodus 24:8). Jesus added that his blood (in view of his death) is **poured out for many**. This outpouring is an essential ritual element in a sacrificial offering and for others. (In the temple sacrifices, the animals' blood had to flow to the ground.)

The symbolism of wine for blood is largely lost by a modern audience. The semitic expression for wine, usually red, was "the blood of the grape." This originates in the wine-making process: people trampled upon the grapes so that they "died" and gave out their "blood." **Truly I tell you, I will never again drink of the fruit of the vine until the day when I drink it new in the kingdom of God**. This final emphatic "amen" statement of Jesus shows his determination to go ahead and his confidence that even if he dies, he will again return to eat and drink with them.

Peter's Denial Foretold

14:26 Any audience past or present finds it hard to accept Jesus' words, **You will all become deserters**. The story shows that despite failures, God will still be faithful, forgive, and continue to work through people. Jesus assures the disciples that even if God allows the good shepherd to be struck down and the sheep scattered, he will return to go before them in Galilee once more.

Peter will not believe this and protests that he will not be like the others. So Jesus has to repeat his prediction and single out Peter.

Jesus Prays in Gethsemane

14:32 This is the agonizing decision time of the passion narrative. It was the last chance for Jesus, under cover of night, to return to Galilee where he had strong support. Yet he knew that God had called him to preach in the Jerusalem capital like Jeremiah and other prophets. Jesus' prayer is a long struggle to make the right decision. More than other gospels, Mark presents this with all the contrasts of human weakness seeking divine strength. Jesus falls prostrate on the ground and prays, **Abba, Father, for you all things are possible; remove this cup from me; yet not what I want, but what you want.**

"Abba," Aramaic for "Father," is the exact word used by Jesus. It is still used in Israel and parts of Syria by children addressing their fathers. The accent is on devotion to God as a faithful child: "Not what I want, but what you want." Jesus repeats these words over and over to gain strength to face his coming arrest.

Three times Jesus returns to his disciples to encourage them to pray, but finds them asleep. This note is for an audience who may also face arrest or suffering if they are faithful to their beliefs. They will fail or desert Jesus like Peter and the twelve unless they pray as Jesus did for divine strength. Finally Jesus feels within him that he has received that strength. He then departs to give himself up voluntarily to Judas and his cohorts coming to arrest him.

The Betrayal and Arrest of Jesus

14:43 The armed crowd, led through the dark night by Judas, quickly arrests Jesus after Judas' pre-arranged treacherous identification kiss. After a brief armed resistance by a disciple, Jesus states that he is not a revolutionary relying on force, power and secrecy. If they arrest him, it is a sign not of weakness but of his desire to do what God asks of him. The same would be true of any of the audience. Mark then records the sad words, **All of them deserted him and fled**. Jesus had expected and even predicted this. However, in this dark atmosphere, the next surprise incident opens up new hope.

A certain young man was following him, wearing nothing but a linen cloth. They caught hold of him, but he left the linen cloth and ran off naked. Yet despite the arrest and the shocking desertion of Jesus' closest disciples, this youth bravely continued to follow. When seized, he escaped naked and embarrassed. He is anonymous to represent those anonymous audience believers who will follow Jesus whatever the risk or danger. He is a mere youth to typify the gospel surprise element regarding children/youth—those "last" but by no means "least." Later we will discover this youth's unusual role at the climax of Mark's drama.

Jesus' Trial Before the Council

14:53 The writer's principal concern is to contrast, for audience reflection, Jesus' heroic confession and Peter's gradual withdrawal and denial. When questioned by authority, Jesus bravely confesses who he is and what he stands for: **the messiah, Son of the Blessed One**. This is the only open confession Jesus makes in this gospel, though it will lead to his death. The previous confession of Peter had not been enough and was before Jesus' teaching about the cross.

The judges of Jesus were a group of priests, scribes and elders. They constituted the puppet religious and political senate, at the head of which was the high priest who was appointed by the Roman governor. The judges needed false witnesses: **Some said they had heard him say, "I will destroy this temple that is made with hands and in three days I will build another, not made with hands**. Jesus had never said these words. Yet they were strangely true for the gospel audience who understood that Jesus' death would make possible a new temple of God. This was also foreshadowed in the temple cleansing story.

In response to his judges, Jesus responded that he would return as the Son of Man and judge to vindicate the truth of his confession to be messiah and Son of God. The high priest then ritually tore his garments as a sign of blasphemy against God.

This blasphemy may have been more evident to the audience than to those actually present at Jesus' trial. By the time Mark wrote, Christian beliefs about Jesus' person had become much more elevated and more a source of friction between Jews and Christians. Yet it is possible that the high priest used blasphemy in the sense that Jesus' claim was an offense and blasphemy to Roman authority through his claim to be a king (messiah, anointed one). Whatever the nature of this blasphemy, Jesus' claim to be messiah constituted a charge that could serve as a basis for trial before the Roman governor who had jurisdiction over such serious matters.

Peter Denies Jesus Three Times

14:66 Intertwined with Jesus' trial by way of contrast is the "trial" of Peter and his gradual weakening under pressure. First he is at a distance in the courtyard. Then he denies to a servant woman that he knew Jesus. In steady progression he denies three times that he was associated with the master. The turning point comes when **Peter remembered** what Jesus had said to him. Jesus had not rejected him though he knew he would fail. **And he broke down and wept.** This is a very moving moment in Mark's gospel for audience identification. The gospel listeners know they could hardly have done worse than Peter, yet Jesus forgave him and even made him his rock and foundation for a future community. The only requirement is to **remember** as Peter did.

PATHWAYS TO FURTHER DISCOVERY:

Carefully compare the text of the anointing at Bethany with the last supper and its context. What conclusions do you draw?

PERSONAL JOURNAL SUGGESTION:

An important road to personal discovery is identification. Imagine how you have been like each of the following at various times and how this can be meaningful to you: the woman at Bethany; the disciples objecting to her; Peter; Judas; Jesus.

Jesus Before Pilate

15:1 The ruling council brings Jesus to Pilate, the Roman governor, for a trial and sentence. There is no question about the nature of this charge, for Pilate asks Jesus, **Are you the king of the Jews?** In other words, a messiah or anointed one, the greatest threat to Roman power. The same title on the cross will suggest the reason for Jesus' execution. All in all, the title occurs six times in this chapter. Rome alone is responsible for the sentencing and execution of Jesus. Expressions like "the Jews killed Jesus" are a horrible travesty of the truth that have caused untold suffering to millions of innocent people through the centuries. Jesus is silent and will not admit the charges. The words, **You say so**, mean that Jesus has not been a messiah in Pilate's sense.

Pilate Condemns Jesus to Crucifixion and Death

15:6 Barabbas was a revolutionary leader who was guilty of murder during a revolt. As such, he awaited execution in prison. Yet the small crowd assembled by the rulers asks for his release rather than that of Jesus. The choice is one for the audience as well. What type of messiah do they want—Jesus, a non-violent messiah of peace, or Barabbas, a leader of violence and power? Barabbas in Aramaic means "son of the father," so the contrast to Jesus is quite evident. **He (Pilate) handed him over to be crucified.** This handing over is not to the Jewish leaders but to the Roman soldiers in the next verse under the command of a Roman centurion (15:39).

The Roman Soldiers Mock Jesus

15:16 The soldiers played a familiar game. This involved dressing up and crowning someone as emperor and making him the object of all kinds of mockery, jokes and cruel, rough treatment. Excavated parts of the original stone pavement and marks on stones for these games have been found. For the audience, some of whom had been soldiers, the contrast is striking: those who bend their knees in mockery will someday actually worship a disgraced, crucified messiah. God's power of turning humiliation and disgrace into triumph is a great joyful surprise to an audience of any time.

The Crucifixion of Jesus

15:21 This account does not furnish the details and descriptions of a modern newspaper. The whole focus is on the meaning of Jesus' death in terms of God's plan in the scriptures. **They compelled a passerby...to carry the cross.** Mark notes this because Simon, an African from the Roman province of Cyrene, is the first person, like Jesus, to carry the cross. He did so unwillingly, yet with a tremendous impact on his own life and others. He became the **father of Alexander and Rufus,** converted Christians known to the audience. The message is forceful: God asks no one to carry the cross with a smile; patient endurance will bring its own unexpected fruit in time and deeply affect others. **Golgotha (which means "place of the skull")** was a familiar place by the road to Jerusalem for frequent public executions and horrible sufferings. **They offered him wine mixed with myrrh but he did not take it.** A drugged wine would have eased his pain, but Jesus chose to be as alert as possible to the end.

And they crucified him and divided his garments among them, casting lots. The details of crucifixion are too horrible for description. Mark selects those illustrating not just that Jesus' death is a frightful tragedy and accident but that God's mysterious transforming plan is at work. The main scripture selected is Psalm 22 on the theme of the suffering and triumph of a just servant of God. In verse 18 of this psalm we find the mention of dividing garments and casting lots. In other words, soldiers appear to do this just to make their customary extra profit. However, beneath their actions the divine plan is at work. **And with him they crucified two bandits, one on his right, one on his left.** These "bandits" were revolutionaries who resorted to violent theft to finance their efforts. To all appearance, Jesus is just another one of them.

While on the cross, three different groups contribute to a last temptation of Christ to prove his cause by power. First of all, the passers-by shake their heads in mocking disbelief. Once again the temple theme recurs, for Jesus will accomplish their taunting remarks in God's mysterious ways: **Aha, you who would destroy the temple and build it in three days, save yourself and us**. What could be more ludicrous than a helpless messiah! The chief priests and scribes take up the same theme, pretending they would be ready to believe if Jesus came down from the cross. The third group is the two others at Jesus' right and left hand.

The Death of Jesus

15:33 **The darkness over the whole land** symbolizes the cosmic significance of Jesus' death, a foreshadowing of his future return as Son of Man (13:24). The evangelist focuses on Jesus' last words in his own language, translated, **My God, my God, why have you forsaken me?**—a quotation from Psalm 22:1. The dark atmosphere of apparently complete abandonment, even by God, is meant for the audience so they can have hope during similar feelings, especially under persecution. The same Psalm 22 has this hope in the second part of its prayer.

Some bystanders misunderstood Jesus' words and thought he was calling on Elijah. For the audience, Elijah was the popular patron of a happy death, since God delivered him from death in a fiery chariot (1 Kings 2:11). Elijah was expected to return to help the just in their last hour (Malachi 4:5). But no Elijah comes to help Jesus, and even this hope turns into derision. Nor will Elijah suddenly intervene for the audience if they face loneliness and abandonment like Jesus.

Then Jesus gave a loud cry and breathed his last. No one would expect such a strong loud cry from someone completely debilitated and ready to die after three hours on the cross. It is a supreme sign of victory despite every appearance of utter failure. The vibrating power of that cry opens up the temple veil and access to divine forgiveness for all. This had been previously an exclusive privilege of the Jewish people. The high priest negotiated this once a year by entering the holy of holies to sprinkle sacrificial blood on the sacred ark of the covenant to obtain forgiveness of sin for the people of Israel (Leviticus 16).

Now when the centurion, who stood facing him, saw that in this way he breathed his last....The above extension of forgiveness to all came first to the most unlikely candidate, a Roman centurion and professional executioner. He had been a hardened and insensitive man, skilled in frequently supervising the most cruel death ever devised by the human race. The manner of Jesus' death so impressed him that he made the climactic confession of faith in the gospel: **Truly this man was God's Son**. Yes, Jesus' death was worthwhile and made a difference by winning over this Roman, a firstfruit and example of many future believers. It tells the audience that all of us can make a real difference and impact on the world if we are willing to risk our lives for what we believe in.

More surprises are ahead for the audience: **There were also women looking on from a distance. Among them were Mary Magdalene** and others who had followed him from Galilee. Their actual names occur three times: here, 15:47 and 16:1. This is important because they are the essential witnesses of Jesus' actual death, place of burial and resurrection. We noted Jesus' first words to his disciples in Galilee: **Follow me and I will make you fish for people** (1:17). Who actually did this? The stalwart twelve had all abandoned him at his arrest. The only ones to follow him all the way from Galilee to the cross were these faithful women. Although the gospel has the atmosphere of a male-dominated world, God does not act that way and turns human expectations upside down. Dedicated women made possible the fishing for people that Jesus promised. Women in the audience can identify with the **many women** that Mark notes in 15:41. These are the first *fisherwomen* who continued Jesus' work.

The Burial of Jesus

15:42 Another effect of Jesus' death was to inspire still others to come out and take a stand. **Joseph of Arimathea** is one of these since he risked his life by claiming Jesus' body. (This would make him suspect to Roman authority as a friend of a revolutionary.) Mark does not call him a disciple but a faithful Jew looking for God's kingdom. Pilate takes care to verify the certainty of Jesus' death. The details of wrapping the corpse and its burial also confirm this reality. **Then Joseph rolled a stone against the door of the tomb.** This symbolizes the seal of death with all its irreversible power.

The Resurrection of Jesus

16:1 When the sabbath was over, Mary Magdalene, and Mary the mother of James, and Salome bought spices, so that they might go and anoint him. On the first Easter Sunday, there was no press corps or television crew to cover the news. The faithful women alone come to the tomb to anoint his dead body as a last loving service. They kept talking to one another about the big problem ahead: **Who will roll away the stone for us from the entrance of the tomb?** But then, when they looked up they were utterly amazed when **they saw that the stone, which was large, had already been moved back.**

And as they entered the tomb, they saw a young man, dressed in a white robe, sitting on the right side; and they were alarmed. To understand what happened, we must focus on Mark's story and not make comparisons to other gospels. The only one who could have rolled away the huge stone is the unlikely youth seated inside! Here is another audience surprise. The youth's description is similar to the youth in 14:50 who had followed Jesus faithfully and ran away naked after he was seized and arrested. The youth also represents the transformation of those who follow Jesus in the same way despite shame and embarrassment. They also can roll back the terrible stone barrier of death and teach others about Jesus' resurrection: **You are looking for Jesus of Nazareth, who was crucified. He has been raised; he is not here.**

Then the youth, seated in the place of authority on the right side of the tomb as a teacher, gives them a final commission: **Go tell his disciples and Peter that he is going ahead of you into Galilee; there you will see him, just as he told you.** Following this, we have a seemingly abrupt ending to the gospel: **They (the women) went out and fled from the tomb, for terror and amazement had seized them; and they said nothing to anyone, for they were afraid.** This puzzling, incomplete ending has always been troublesome for almost two thousand years. Everyone likes to have a complete, happy, triumphant end to a story of a hero.

To remedy this, ancient copyists added a variety of endings to the gospel, with many details taken from other gospels. (See your New Testament text notations.) Thousands of scholars have also struggled to interpret Mark's ending in a more favorable light. However why not just accept that Mark wanted the ending incomplete? Perhaps the women somehow failed to get the message to Peter and the disciples. So it still remains to be done by the audience with the assurance that Jesus will go before them as a good shepherd so they can begin again his ministry in Galilee and await his second coming: **There you will see him as he told you**.

PATHWAYS TO FURTHER DISCOVERY:

Compare Mark 5:1–20 (the cure of the Gerasene demoniac) with Mark 14:51–52 and 16:1–5. How does the Gerasene story foreshadow the gospel ending?

PERSONAL JOURNAL SUGGESTION:

The gospel begins with the theme of new beginnings/youth/childhood at the Jordan River. The theme continues through Jesus' illustrations and teachings on the meaning of the child. The gospel ends with the youth again as a symbol of perpetual youth. What implications does this have for your own life-style and spirituality?

PART II
THE JESUS STORY:
THE VOICE OF MATTHEW

Introduction to Matthew

We can best understand why Matthew wrote by comparisons with Mark regarding audience, time and setting. We have seen that Mark addressed a mostly Greek, non-Jewish audience to whom he had to explain Jewish customs, words and names. In contrast, Matthew does not need to do this. He even presumes that his listeners are still observing all the customs and laws of the Jewish Torah.

In Mark, the atmosphere was that of a community under severe Roman persecution. There is still some of this in Matthew. However, the main difficulty is between Jewish Christians and their Jewish brothers and sisters. These difficulties arose especially in the years after the Jewish war with Rome (66–71 A.D.). On the Christian side, there was considerable development in their views about Jesus, whom they looked upon increasingly as a divine Son of God. This was extremely difficult to imagine by fellow Jews who held strongly to monotheism as central to their faith.

On the Jewish side, with the destruction of Jerusalem and priestly authority, the Pharisees increasingly dominated Judaism so that their leadership, teaching and example became normative for most Jews. This also resulted in increasing friction with Jewish Christians who no longer felt welcome in Jewish synagogues and society. Another difficulty for Jewish Christians was the fact that they were gradually becoming a minority within largely Gentile communities. These latter did not share the total dedication of their Jewish Christian members to the Torah and Jewish traditions.

Consequently, Jewish Christians faced a crisis regarding their future. Where should they turn for authority and direction? The following were possible paths they could take. 1) They could return to their former revered teachers and models, the Pharisees. 2) They could go off and establish independent purely Jewish-Christian communities with their own authority and customs. History tells us that some of them did this and established their own communities across the Jordan. 3) They could follow the advice in Matthew's gospel by accepting new authority in Peter and his successors and adopt God's plan for a broadening Gentile apostolate.

Time is also an important factor in Matthew. In Mark, we saw that time was running out for Jesus' return. In face of persecution, actions were supremely important—especially being ready to suffer and even give your life for your faith. However, Matthew faces the problem that Jesus has not returned as quickly as expected. So he concentrates on Jesus' words and teachings regarding practical everyday life.

Time is also a factor that pushes Matthew to give more attention to the institutional aspects of the community Jesus has established. Mark wrote little of this because he thought Jesus was returning soon. However Matthew must explain how Jesus' presence continues in the community through the tradition of his teachings and through authoritative teachers.

The Sources of Matthew

Matthew, according to most scholars, wrote after Mark, toward the end of the first century. Matthew used Mark's gospel, or the tradition behind it, for one of his sources. In fact, about ninety percent of Mark, in some form or other, is in Matthew. However the latter gospel is about fifty percent longer than Mark and uses other sources also. One of these is a source of materials that are also in Luke, but not in Mark or John. Scholars call this "Q," an abbreviation of the German *Quelle*, meaning "source." In addition, there is a large portion of Matthew found nowhere else in the gospels. This proper material is very valuable for finding the special goals and intentions of the author.

Knowledge of the above sources will help us in our study of Matthew. As we go along, we will note how Matthew adapts materials he has taken from Mark. We will compare how Matthew and Luke treat passages found only in "Q." We will give more attention to stories and traditions found only in Matthew. At the beginning of each study section, we will note these parallels for reference.

SUGGESTIONS FOR STUDY

Start by reading the whole gospel of Matthew in one or two sittings. As you go along, note what strikes you as you make a first comparison with Mark. Especially notice how the person of Jesus emerges in each gospel. Then as you study each passage, look up the parallels to the other gospels indicated. A good reference to easily do this is a book called *Gospel Parallels* that has the first three gospels side by side for comparison (see Bibliography).

The Gospel According to Matthew

The story of Jesus' origins and birth in chapters 1 and 2 announces central themes important for the whole gospel. Like similar ancient birth and childhood accounts, they presuppose and include the whole life of the hero, in this case Jesus the messiah, son of God.

The Genealogy of Jesus the Messiah

1:1 This genealogy brings out the distinguished Jewish roots of Jesus in descending from Abraham their father and David the king. God had promised David (around 1000 B.C.) that his dynasty would never fail and that there would always be kings from his descendants (2 Samuel 7:11). Later prophetic hopes focused on a single anointed one (*messiah*, in Hebrew) as a special source of hope, particularly in times of crisis.

However, on close examination, the lineage of Jesus is seriously flawed! David the king had committed both murder and adultery (1:6–7). Rahab (5) had been a prostitute. Judah had fathered twins by incest through Tamar (3). Ruth a foreigner and Gentile was the grandmother of David. Matthew tells us here and through his gospel that God works his plans even through the most evil and scandalous human conduct. God works not only despite evil but even through it when necessary.

The Birth of Jesus

1:18 The most shocking scandal of all appears in stories about Jesus' birth. (Later we will see evidence of similar stories about Jesus' resurrection in 28:11–15.) Mary, Jesus' mother, was engaged to be married to Joseph. However, this was not like a modern engagement. It was actually a marriage contract, yet it was not customary for the couple to begin living together until after the wedding celebration, which might be many months afterward.

Joseph was stunned to find out that his bride had become pregnant and he knew the child was not his. Consequently, he was planning to give her papers of divorce according to the biblical laws of Deuteronomy 24:1. In the biblical tradition, important messages come from God during times of prayer and agonizing decisions. Another Joseph, the son of Jacob, had many divine communications through dreams (Genesis 37–41).

Similarly, Joseph in the New Testament had a dream in which an angel told him, **Joseph, son of David, do not be afraid to take Mary as your wife, for the child conceived in her is from the Holy Spirit.** Joseph obeyed the angel and did so, thus taking the child as his own in the public domain. He also made possible the fulfillment of scripture that Jesus should be a son of David since the genealogy is that of Joseph, not Mary.

You are to name him Jesus, for he will save his people from their sins. The name "Jesus" is actually Greek, but derived from the Hebrew, "Joshua," rooted in the verb "save." Jesus' name summarizes his mission to save people from any future judgment through present forgiveness.

Throughout his gospel, Matthew will be quoting scriptures to encourage his predominantly Jewish-Christian audience by showing the fulfillment of God's plans. A central theme in Matthew will be **Emmanuel, which means, "God is with us."** (Emmanuel in abbreviated form is the origin of "Noel" in French.) God will be with his people in the birth and life of Jesus. At the gospel ending, the theme continues as the risen Jesus announces, **I will be with you**—that he will always be with his disciples until the end of time.

A virgin shall conceive and bear a son. After all the unusual births in Jesus' genealogy, including that of Isaac to

Abraham and Sarah (1:2) in their old age, this is the most miraculous of all. It announces the greatness of this son in accord with the prophecy of Isaiah 7:10–14.

The Visit of the Magi

2:1 These childhood stories are largely what is called "midrash." This Hebrew term means a meditative weaving together of biblical texts and traditions to discover the meaning of events in God's plan. Jesus' birth and childhood will foreshadow his whole career, especially the triumphant ending of his life despite rejection and apparent failure. Here the mysterious visit of the **wise men from the east** foreshadows the gospel ending and Jesus' commission to bring the gospel to all nations (28:16–20).

The magi follow a **star**, perhaps a reference to Numbers 24:19, **A star shall come out of Jacob**. The kings take a long journey of faith to reach King Herod of Israel. Then the paradox is striking: Herod, despite his deceit and evil intentions, actually directs the magi to Bethlehem! (The Matthean theme that God even turns evil into good.) On finding the child's home, **the wise men were overwhelmed with joy**. This is the messianic joy the audience experiences in knowing that God lavishes his gifts even on strangers and outsiders. The kings offer him appropriate gifts for a royal child—**gold, frankincense, and myrrh**. These gifts symbolize the joyful tribute of the whole world. This is because Psalm 77:10–15 uses similar words to describe the gifts that the kings of the world bring to Israel's king.

The Flight into Egypt

2:13 **Take the child and his mother and flee to Egypt.** In this brief chapter 2, there are nine references to **the child** or **the child and his mother**. "The child" is a reference to the promised child of Isaiah 9:6: **A child has been born for us**. The image of mother and child is important for Matthew's audience of any time as a source of hope and joy. **Egypt** is not only a place but a recurring symbol of suffering and identification. All Jews had to learn what Egypt meant in order to identify with their people's history. Matthew has a strong identification theme in his gospel: Jesus, at least symbolically, has to go to Egypt and be identified with people's needs and sufferings.

The Massacre of the Innocents

2:16 This story has striking parallels to Moses' infancy where the pharaoh of Egypt sought to kill all male children to limit Israel's growing population. In this gospel, Jesus will be like a new Moses who leads his people out of "Egypt" and gives them a new covenant. Continuing the Moses parallel, an angel comes to Joseph in a dream, saying, **Go to the land of Israel, for those who were seeking the child's life are dead**. God also spoke similar words to Moses telling him to return to Egypt after the death of the pharaoh (Exodus 4:19–20). Jesus' new home becomes Nazareth. Matthew even finds an ingenious prophecy interpretation to go with this: **He will be called a Nazarene**. This may be a reference to the nazirite vow of consecration to God (Judges 13:4–5).

The Preaching of John the Baptist

3:1 (See Mark 1:1–8.) **When he (John) saw many Pharisees and Sadducees coming for baptism.** With these words and what follows, Matthew adds to Mark a strong warning not to merely follow old religious leaders but to embark on a new path of repentance. Matthew also sharpens the distinction between Jesus and the Baptist by omitting the Markan mention of forgiveness of sins in John's baptism (Mark 1:14). Instead he has this forgiveness of sins inserted in the last supper in connection with Jesus' death (26:28). This will be part of Matthew's stronger Christological outlook in his gospel.

Matthew further adds the word **fire** to describe Jesus' baptism. The image of fire conveys refining and transformation. This gospel also has a fiery picture of the Baptist as a stern prophet bringing people to judgment and decision. His image of Jesus conforms to this model: he separates wheat from chaff and destroys the latter with unquenchable fire. John is a sterner and more powerful figure than in Mark's gospel. Matthew will stress judgment, rewards and punishments more than any other gospel in order to lead audiences to decision.

The Baptism of Jesus

3:13 (See Mark 1:9–11.) In Matthew, John is reluctant to baptize Jesus. This may be due to the existence of disciples of the Baptist scattered over the world even after Jesus' death. Some of them never became full believers in Jesus (Acts 18:24–19:7). It was necessary to show that Jesus was in no way inferior to the Baptist though apparently so by being baptized by him. Jesus goes to John's baptism **to fulfill all righteousness**. In chapter 1, the name of Jesus meant that he was to save sinners. To save them, he must be at their side in the Jordan River.

In Mark, Jesus hears God speaking privately to him, "You are my Son." In Matthew, God directs his voice to the reader, presenting Jesus to them: **This is my Son, the Beloved**. In this gospel there are only a few relics of Mark's messianic secret. The baptism of Jesus is clearly public and meant for all. Jesus establishes the path of righteousness for everyone by stepping first into the waters of repentance.

PATHWAYS TO FURTHER DISCOVERY:

Compare the first three chapters of Matthew with the last two. How does the beginning of Matthew prepare the way for its end?

PERSONAL JOURNAL SUGGESTION:

Like Joseph in the New and Old Testament, you may have significant dreams at times. In each day's journal, note the dreams you have and what meaning they could have for you.

The Temptation of Jesus

4:1 (See Mark 1:12–13.) **If you are the Son of God.** The Son of God title at Jesus' baptism leads Jesus and the audience to a decision about the meaning that title has in their lives. The three temptations closely parallel the three last temptations of Christ on the cross beginning with the same words, "If you are the Son of God (27:40). The tempter only knows the way of power: **Command these stones to become bread**. Jesus replies that people live by the creative word of God that is underneath all bread. Jesus follows that word/plan, not the way of power.

The second temptation goes a little further—to trust that God will save him from suffering and death. The third is on a **very high mountain**. It introduces Matthew's favorite mountain image. Repeatedly, the bible recalls the fiery mountain of Sinai where God gave his commandments amid thunder and lightning. Of course, it is Jesus' mission to bring the world to God. The devil claims that he can make it a reality by worshiping him (following his plan). Jesus replies with the words of the first commandment, that he can only follow his Father's way. That plan will bring all the world to him as we will see in the final mountain scene at the end of Matthew's gospel (28:16–20). However, the way to this will be God's own secret plan of the cross.

Jesus Begins His Ministry in Galilee

4:12 (See Mark 1:14–15.) Repent, **the kingdom of heaven** has come near. Mark always has, "The kingdom of *God*." Matthew retains the original Jewish flavor where "heaven" is a way of avoiding God's name (out of reverence). God is the one who "is in heaven," as in the Lord's prayer. Heaven means "sky," which the ancients considered as the top of the universe, from which stars hung like chandeliers. People imagined that God dwelt in heaven or just above the heavens. It was a way of declaring that God was above and beyond all earthly creation. Matthew's language and atmosphere bring us much closer to the original setting of Jesus' words—although Mark is a much more exciting storyteller.

Jesus Calls His First Disciples

4:18 (See Mark 1:16–20.) **Simon who is called Peter.** Matthew's first mention of Peter adds his new name (see 16:16–20). We already noted in the introduction to Matthew his different time perspective. No longer expecting Jesus to shortly return, Matthew is much more concerned with continuity, succession and the institutions to make this possible. Peter will be a founding rock of the continuing community. Replacing the Jerusalem authorities, Peter and other teachers like him will have Jesus' presence and authority with them as they continue his work and teaching.

Jesus Teaches and Heals in Galilee

4:23 This widening of Jesus' ministry to borderline largely Gentile areas introduces the Sermon on the Mount and its wider audience.

The Sermon on the Mount
(Matthew, 5–7; see Luke 6:20–49)

Matthew's gospel centers about five neatly defined discourses: 1) the sermon on the mount; 2) the apostolic instruction (10:1–11:1); 3) the parables (13:1–53); 4) church discipline (18:1–19:1); 5) the eschatological discourse (24:1–26:1). While Mark stressed Jesus' actions for imitation, Matthew focuses more on Jesus' words and teachings which mediate his power and continued presence in the community/church.

The most important of the five great discourses is the sermon on the mount which is Matthew's compendium of Jesus' teaching. The collection goes far beyond anything in its original setting. Actually, it includes things said on other occasions in the other gospels. Not only that, the collection goes beyond Jesus' earthly life and presupposes his death, resurrection and presence in his church.

The atmosphere of the sermon is not legalistic or restrictive. It presupposes "amazing grace" and the resulting costs of discipleship. The poetic form of Jesus' sayings made them easy to memorize and hand down for decades before they were put into written form for reference. The idea was not to simply remember information but to be continually renewed and energized. People took the words to heart as spoken to them as a live audience by a living risen Jesus.

The Beatitudes

5:1 **When Jesus saw the crowds, he went up the mountain.**
This is Matthew's favorite mountain theme. The fiery Mount
Sinai is in the background where God gave his commandments
to his people through Moses. Here Jesus is enthroned (sits
down) with divine authority like a new Moses to give his own
commandments to his people. The beatitudes are the keynote
introduction providing a new interior basis for a meaningful life
in contrast to the exterior things most people find so important.

**Blessed are the poor in spirit, for theirs is the kingdom of
heaven.** The beatitudes get their name from the opening word
"beatus" of the Latin translation of "blessed" or "happy." Most
people connect happiness with the "luck" to have exterior things
such as money, power, recognition, sex, etc. Jesus' teaching
focuses *within*. The **poor in spirit** is a biblical reference to those
who need God and not money to fill their desires. Thus, they
have everything they need and the kingdom of heaven is theirs.

Those that mourn are those who feel sorry not for themselves but for others. With real compassion they sympathize
with the sufferings of other people. **They shall be comforted.**
This and other parallels are in the passive voice in the typical
Jewish way of avoiding direct mention of God. Thus we would
say, "God will comfort them." The beatitudes have a strong
future orientation. A present path of selflessness makes possible
a future deep and permanent joy. **Blessed are the meek.** The
meek are those who renounce violence and control over others.
In return, God gives them the whole earth as a gift. "Inheriting
the earth" is symbolic of God's gifts since he had promised the
land to his people Israel.

Those who hunger and thirst for righteousness are people
whose real inner desire or "hunger" is God's justice for
everyone, though this means that at times they will choose to
have less so that others will have enough. God will fill their
desires and hunger. **The merciful** are those like God whose great
name is "the Merciful One." Being like God, they receive this
mercy themselves in the fullest measure.

The pure of heart. In the bible, the heart is the source of
intention and desire. Matthew will emphasize this throughout
his gospel. Where the heart is simple, uncluttered and pure,

people will be able to really see God with perfect eyesight. **The peacemakers.** Peace, *shalom* in Hebrew, sums up every blessing from God, especially that of reconciliation (5:23–26). **Children of God** is often in the sense of imitation—someone who is like a parent, in this case, God.

Those who are persecuted. (See introduction on friction between Jews and Jewish Christians.) **Rejoice and be glad**—the surprising and "ridiculous" response of those who become grace-filled and like the Merciful One. It is rejoicing not from a love of suffering itself (nowhere praised in scripture) but rooted in being a bearer of God's message which has brought sufferings on many prophets.

The Images of Salt and Light

5:13 Jesus' teachings are meant for everyone. The mission of a disciple is to provide a *flavor* to the whole earth and a spark/light to the world. Their salt is not just to sprinkle on themselves but to use for others. **Let your light shine before others.** This is God's light and will be recognized by others and draw them to God. Here is another Matthean theme—that outsiders will be our judges as they observe and see what we do (25:31–46).

Jesus and the Law and Prophets

5:17 **Do not think that I have come to abolish the law or the prophets.** Jesus does not ask Jewish Christians to abandon their traditional cultural and religious practices. His teaching respects cultural diversity but goes beyond it. **Unless your righteousness exceeds that of the scribes and Pharisees.** These were respected teachers and models for many in the audience. However Jesus will present a challenge to go even beyond them so they will not be tempted to return to their former teachers.

You have heard that it was said...but I say to you. Jesus begins to present how his teachings will lead them to new heights of perfection superior to that of past teachers just mentioned. What they "heard that it was said" was God's thunderous voice giving the ten commandments on

Mount Sinai. "I say to you" is now God's voice through Jesus providing a new inner basis and motivation behind the ten commandments.

Teaching on Anger and Violence

5:21 **You shall not murder** is the fifth commandment which everyone knows, yet is not sufficient to prevent killing and violence. Jesus immediately goes to the inner roots of murder and violence. The first is a lack of meaningful personal relationships. So Jesus repeats the words, **your brother (and sister)** some seven times in this chapter. The second root is **anger**. From the context, this is not just a passing feeling but a deep unresolved hatred in the heart. It comes to the surface in insulting words, lack of personal respect and sensitivity toward others.

To resolve these causes of murder and violence, Jesus elevates forgiveness to the highest religious duty, beyond that of a **gift at the altar**. This is illustrated by a humorous extreme: If an unresolved anger comes to a person's memory even in the middle of a religious ceremony, he or she should immediately drop everything, go out and seek a reconciliation. **Come to terms quickly with your accuser while you are on the way to court with him.** Jesus advocates a Jewish teaching that opponents should take the long walk to a court case together. This is so they could dialogue, make their own terms and not wait for a judge's decision that could be harsh and costly for everyone concerned.

Teaching on Adultery

5:27 The well-known sixth commandment likewise does not seem to be enough to curb sexual excesses. Jesus again goes to the inner roots, a lack of personal respect, and a relationship that regards another person as a mere object of pleasure. **Everyone who looks at a woman with lust has already committed adultery with her in his heart.** This is quite different from thoughts or imagination about sex. It is something deep in the heart and intention that moves toward the abusive actions next described.

If your right eye causes you to sin...or...if your right hand causes you to sin. The remedy must be decisive: **tear it out...cut it off**. These are typical oriental exaggerations but they mean to take immediate remedial action when facing occasions of sin. In Mark 9:46, we saw the reference to **gehenna** or hell. However, the many references to future rewards and punishments in Matthew prompt us to believe that he wrote down Jesus' words in the sense of future punishment.

Teaching on Divorce
5:31 (See Mark 10:1–12 and Matthew 19:1–12)

Teaching on Oaths and Swearing

5:33 Here Jesus moves to the eighth commandment concerning false witness and untruth. Casuistry was popular in ancient times as it is today, used to try to find out the boundaries between right and wrong. Jesus advocates a new Christian language that does not rely on oaths and expletives to try to convince or impress others. **Let your word be "Yes, Yes," or "No, No."** Here again the inner cure is trustfulness that relies on a simplicity of words and expressions.

Teaching on Violence and Retaliation

5:38 **An eye for an eye and a tooth for a tooth** from Exodus 21:24. This has often been interpreted literally and out of context. Originally it tried to guarantee a just legal recompense (usually in money or other exchange), not a terrible vengeance. Jesus responds, **Do not resist the evildoer**. This refers to people who are hurtful and insulting because of believers' faith in Jesus (5:11). Jesus does not call for passivity but a spirit and direction of life that overcomes evil by good instead of retaliation. The expression "to turn the other cheek" has even entered the English language. It is meant to humorously express that we should not simply reply to evil with evil. Some of the humor in Jesus' words has been lost unless we translated his next expression by "If someone wants to sue you in court and take your coat, let that person take your pants also!"

If anyone forces you to go one mile, go along the second. People in the empire well knew what this meant as Roman soldiers requisitioned civilians to carry their heavy baggage under the hot sun. The ordinary response at the end of the required mile was seething anger and at least a silent curse. The humorous response of "flower people" is to smile and say, "Could I help you for another mile?" **Give to those who ask you.** These are not polite beggars but rude pushy ones—a real test for cheerful generosity. We would like them to politely ask for favors, not press us with just demands for their human rights to food, clothing and shelter. "Giving" is its own reward. Those who feel they are receiving justice, not favors, often do not express gratitude.

Love for One's Enemies

5:43 **You shall love your neighbor and hate your enemy.** This is not in the bible but is a common saying or proverb. Matthew's gospel is very practical. What can be done with recurring, gnawing thoughts of hurtful people? The answer is simple and humorous: "retaliate" by sending love and energy through prayer. Yet this is so difficult for weak human nature that Jesus provides a new resource: **that you may be children of your Father in heaven.**

This last statement is the central motivation of the sermon on the mount. **Children** here refers to those who are similar to and imitate their heavenly parent. The ideal can then become a reality because children share their parents' power. Imitation of God was the highest ideal of Jewish piety. Here it comes from watching God in nature bestow his gifts of sun and rain on everyone, despite their actions. God's love is *unconditional*—not based on a recipient's merit. The theme of love for the "good and bad" will continue through Matthew.

Be perfect, therefore, as your heavenly Father is perfect. This does not mean to be a "perfectionist." It means someone who is continually growing and maturing as a real child of God. Growth involves learning through experience—which is a nice way of saying "through mistakes." This is the way that Peter and the apostles grew also.

Concerning Almsgiving

6:1 Jesus' concern for the *inner* basis of religion now examines prayer, almsgiving, fasting and money. Privacy was not easy to obtain in the small houses and crowded streets of the poor. There was much public prayer as people stopped to pray during fixed times such as the hours of temple sacrifice. In a world without banks, checkbooks and credit cards, donations were placed in public collection boxes and were observed by many bystanders. Jesus says, **Do not let your left hand know what your right hand is doing.** This is a comic paradox to express the necessity of not parading good works to win the esteem of others.

Concerning Prayer

6:5 Believers are not to imitate the endless repetition of some religious people who try to "force" the hand of God to get what they want. This is really just a form of magic. Instead, their attitude is to be one of complete trust: **Your Father knows what you need before you ask him**. Jesus introduces the "Lord's prayer" with these words, **Pray in this manner.** This is not a formula, but Jesus' own way of prayer which we will later see at Gethsemane (26:36–46). See also Luke 11:1–44.

Hallowed be your name. The word "hallow" now makes its rare appearance at "Halloween," meaning "holy evening." It is rooted in God's creation of each person to his own image and likeness (Genesis 1:27). As such, we mirror God's image to the world in everything we do. So we pray to present a pure image of God to the world and not disgrace it by giving people the wrong idea of what our Father and creator is like.

Your kingdom come. The Lord's prayer is outwardly directed in its concerns—that we may do our best to make God rule in the world through justice, mercy and peace. **Your will be done.** This was Jesus' own prayer before his arrest when he distinguished between what he wanted and what his Father wanted. His prayer was **not what I want but what you want** (27:39). It is extraordinary to ask *not* to get what we want.

Give us this day our daily bread. Bread and food are often taken for granted. Yet Jesus, according to Jewish custom, never ate without a prayer of blessing or acknowledgement (14:19). The blessing pointed to a higher meaning for bread—that God is really the creator and source of all nourishment. Jesus also will give bread a new meaning at his last supper.

Forgive us our debts. Jesus, in story form, will describe sin as a debt or lack of return to God for lending people his gifts. Yet in his mercy he is willing to forgive this (18:23–35). **As we also have forgiven our debtors.** This literal translation of the Greek differs from the common church version, "As we forgive…" Thus, our willingness to forgive others is a necessary receptive quality for God's forgiveness. This is explicit in 18:35 and in 6:14–15.

And do not bring us to the time of trial (temptation). These words are the same as those addressed by Jesus to his sleepy disciples in the garden temptation scene (26:41). There Jesus gives the reason: "The spirit indeed is willing but the flesh is weak." Temptation will bring failure (as was true with the disciples who fled in the garden) if there is not intense prayer like that of Jesus.

But rescue us from the evil one. The devil or Satan is behind temptation according to stories in Jewish tradition. One such account is found in the New Testament in Revelation 12:7–9. There we find the story that there was a revolt among God's angels in heaven. As a result, the rebellious angels were driven down to earth where they tempt people to abandon God's ways.

Concerning Fasting

6:16 By way of background, prayer for the ancients was a very total affair. They used bodily gestures such as raising their hands, lifting their eyes and praying aloud. To give greater intensity to their prayer, they often fasted or gave up sleep. When this was exaggerated, they were quite a sad, though impressive sight. Jesus, laughingly, even advised his disciples to pretend to be feasting rather than fasting to avoid ostentation and people's good impressions.

Treasures on Earth or in Heaven?

6:19 With no bank accounts in those days, people often hid money and precious goods under a house or in a wall in order to save for the future. But all material goods are perishable, and according to biblical tradition, money spent for God's purposes mysteriously multiplies. Matthew's concern here and through his gospel is the intention of the heart: **Where your treasure is there your heart will be also.**

Sound Eyes and Intentions

6:22 The image of the heart and treasure leads to another, that of eyesight. Poor vision blurs everything that we see.

Who Is Your Master, God or Money?

6:24 Matthew likes to present groups of two for audience choice and involvement. Service to God is total by its nature and cannot survive along with worship of money. While we rarely use the term "master," the word "addict" is similar, coming from the root "dictator." This is really something or someone that is telling us what to do and taking God's place.

Cures for Worry and Anxiety

6:25 Continuing the wealth discussion, the reason why many people accumulate money is worry or fear for the future. Jesus' responses are: 1) **Is not life more than food?** Life itself comes from God as a gift and cannot be controlled. 2) All of nature is a constant display of God's care for the least creature, whether plants or animals. 3) **Strive first for the kingdom of God.** With "first things first," everything else is viewed in perspective. 4) **Do not worry about tomorrow, for tomorrow will have worries of its own.** The big secret is to live fully one day at a time. Over ninety percent of worries concern a tomorrow that does not yet exist. As a model for regarding nature as a teacher, Jesus presents the wisdom tradition of **Solomon in all his glory** (see 1 Kings 3–4).

On Judging Others

7:1 **Do not judge.** In view of Jewish avoidance of God's name, the second part would be, "that God may not judge you." Preoccupation with criticizing others means taking God's place but lacking his compassion and neglecting self-criticism. The attitude of searching for specks or flaws in others blinds our eyes from appreciating, like God, the good in others. Yet Jesus adds balancing statements to avoid the danger of completely ignoring the faults of others(6). The sacred community gifts of God are not to be profaned by giving them to those obviously unfit and unappreciative. The "Doctrine on the Twelve Apostles," an early Christian document, applies this to the eucharist.

Obtaining Answers to Prayers

7:7 To emphasize the importance of prayer, Jesus uses a triple image and then repeats it in another form. In oral teaching, the more important a matter is, the more often it is repeated. Perseverance and complete trust is the strong message: "Keep on asking; keep on searching; keep on knocking." **If you...know how to give good gifts to your children, how much more will your Father in heaven give good things.** This is a central revelation of Jesus that God is kinder than any possible human parent, indeed kinder than all of them combined. As such, Matthew's frequent mention of rewards and punishments must be seen in perspective. Jesus did not come on earth just to teach about heaven and hell. This was already part of Jewish traditional teaching and is also found in other religions as well.

The Golden Rule

7:12 **Do to others** is even found in the dictionary under "golden rule." Jesus, however, made it into a summary of all religion. This gospel is very insistent on "doing." This is a verb repeated again and again, leading to a climax in the final judgment scene in 25:31–46. The last part, **As you would have them do to you,** sums up Jesus' identification with others, another central gospel interest. This moves toward the final gospel teaching statement, **just as you did not do it to one of the least of these, you did not do it to me** (25:45).

The Narrow Gate

7:13 Once again, two roads and two choices. The cost of discipleship requires a serious decision. The human tendency is to take the easy way out.

Recognizing True Teachers

7:15 Two types of teacher/shepherds. Some look good in appearances and smooth words, but inwardly they only want to use and devour their sheep/students like lamb chops! The only real credential for a teacher is good, fruitful action.

The Dangers of Self-Deception

7:21 **Not everyone who says to me "Lord, Lord" will enter.** "Lord, Lord" (*Kyrie, Kyrie* in Greek) is an address of Christian prayer to Jesus. Here we have the case of apparently devout believers who pray repeatedly, prophesy and even work miracles in the name of Jesus. Yet they hear the shocking reply to their prayers: **I never knew you; go away from me, you evildoers.** Another example of *orthopraxis* in Matthew: right actions are supremely important rather than religious activity alone.

Conclusion: Hearers and Doers

7:24 Everyone who hears these words of mine and acts on them. These words and the following illustration of a truly **wise person** conclude Jesus' sermon on the mount. Without hearing and doing, discipleship lasts as long as a sandcastle. **Now when Jesus had finished saying these things.** This is a literary ending. Similar statements conclude each of the five great discourses in Matthew. **He taught them as having authority.** Jesus is like Moses, but superior. This authority is a central issue in Matthew. It leads to the gospel ending and "graduation ceremony." There on a mountain platform Jesus will hand over this same teaching authority to others who will bring his teachings to the world accompanied by Jesus' presence and power.

PATHWAYS TO FURTHER DISCOVERY:

The sermon on the mount was designed for easy memory so it could be absorbed and frequently repeated for personal use and for teaching. Memorize twenty or more verses of your choice. What insights came to you through this?

PERSONAL JOURNAL SUGGESTION:

What is "unconditional love" as found in the sermon on the mount? Note each day some practical opportunities to practice this.

TEN MIRACLES AND DISCIPLESHIP (CHAPTERS 8–10)

These prepare the way for the next collection, the apostolic discourse in chapter 10. Matthew's treatment of miracles tells us much about his purposes. Compared with Mark, the same stories are usually much shorter, eliminating many details. Matthew highlights Jesus' *words*. The miracles become more like encounters with Jesus to serve as an audience model. Mark is more "theological," in the sense of being God-centered; Jesus, by his example, leads people to faith in God. Matthew is more "Christological," leading the audience to faith in Jesus. This development came about in the twenty or so years between the two gospels. Also, Matthew emphasizes Jesus' motivation in the miracles—for example, his compassion, identification with others, and fulfillment of scriptures.

Jesus Cleanses and Heals a Leper

8:1 (See Mark 1:40–45.) Matthew omits Jesus' order not to tell anyone. Mark's messianic secret is greatly diluted in Matthew. Everything is more open right from Jesus' baptism.

Jesus Heals a Centurion's Servant

8:5 This story illustrates a Matthean objective: to move his Jewish-Christian audience away from exclusivism to an ideal new community of both Jews and Gentiles. **Lord, I am not worthy to have you come under my roof.** These words sum up the obstacle to that goal. The Roman centurion knows the misgivings a Jewish teacher would have about entering a Gentile home and accepting hospitality. However, Jesus' word from a distance reaches audiences even separated by space and time. (See comments on Mark 7:24–30.)

The story also brings out the power of Jesus' **word** and **authority**. The amazement of Jesus about the foreigner's faith is meant to be echoed by the audience and prepare for the concluding unusual and even comic image: **Many will come from the east and west and will eat with Abraham and Isaac and Jacob.** This is an unthinkable joyful banquet of the Jewish patriarchs sitting at a feast with a horde of outsiders from all over the world. It is comic because no one could possibly imagine such a get-together of their Jewish ancestors with all these ritually unwashed, pork-eating, uncircumcised Gentiles.

The heirs of the kingdom will be thrown into outer darkness. The evangelist writes this for those Jewish Christians in the audience who want to keep their exclusive status. Matthew warns them that they must be open to the new all-inclusive direction of God's plan. The image is that of a brightly candle-lit banquet hall in contrast to the dark streets outside.

Jesus Heals Many at Peter's House

8:14 (See Mark 1:29–34.) Comparing to Mark: Matthew uses the name **Jesus** much more often in view of the opening gospel emphasis. Here it is Jesus' initiative to cure, not the apostles'. *Peter*, his new name, is preferred to *Simon*. After being cured, the mother-in-law began to serve *him*, the person of Jesus, not "them" as in Mark.

The Costs of Discipleship

8:18 Illustrations of the cost and priority of discipleship—a great area of importance for Matthew, who is always using that term. The request to **bury my father** is not to attend a funeral, which would be a religious obligation. It is to stay at home with aging parents until they died.

Jesus Stills the Storm

8:23 (See Mark 4:35–41.) **Lord, save us; we are perishing** is more a community prayer in Matthew—one an audience could use. This community/church emphasis is typical. The address is to the *Lord* rather than the *teacher* in Mark.

Jesus Heals the Gadarene Demoniacs

8:28 (See Mark 5:1–20.) Here we have only one third of the space given by Mark! Matthew has two demons, as he will later have two blind men instead of "one" in Mark. The author likes pairs for a more representative effect. He omits the final commission of the former demoniac that climaxed Mark's story. This is because Matthew does not envision a Gentile apostolate until after Jesus' resurrection (see Matthew 10:5–6; 28:16–20).

Jesus Heals and Cures a Paralytic

9:1 (See Mark 2:1–12.) Very similar to Mark but much abbreviated. Note the double mention of Jesus' *authority*.

The Call of Matthew

9:14 (See Mark 2:13–17.) Readers get a surprise when Matthew (the writer or his source) raises his head at the tax collector's desk instead of Levi in Mark. Matthew also calls himself a tax collector in the apostles' list in 10:3. Certainly, Matthew could have been, as a trained scribe, a tax collector also. We are left with a mystery and the need of detective work! Luke also has Levi there (5:27–32) and does not call Matthew a tax collector in his apostles' list (6:15). Even Matthew does not write that the dinner takes place in his house, while Mark writes that it was in Levi's house. We are left with the suspicion that Matthew may have inserted himself in the story as some artists do in their own paintings. He may have done this to present himself as a humble "sinner"—as bad as a tax collector!

Feasting or Fasting in the Kingdom of God?

9:14 (See Mark 2:18–22.) Matthew presents a sharper contrast to the Baptist's ascetic approach by having the latter's disciples ask the question directly.

Death and Life in the Stories of Two Women

9:18 (See Mark 5:21–43.) Notice the characteristic heightening of the miraculous element in the cures, omitting Mark's detail that the girl had been still alive when Jesus was first called. The evangelist draws more attention to the power of Jesus as healer, omitting or softening down the faith of the recipients. It is Jesus' *word* that cures rather than the woman drawing out Jesus' power as in Mark.

Jesus Heals Two Blind Men

9:27 (See Mark 8:22–26.) Matthew has two blind men to Mark's one to help the reader be the other blind person and thus use together the plural prayer of invocation: **Have mercy on us, Son of David**.

Jesus Heals a Mute Person

9:32 The last opposing statement of the Pharisees in 9:34 serves as an introductory contrast to Jesus' mission as a shepherd/leader and his care to appoint new leaders.

The Twelve Apostles

10:1 (See Mark 3:13–19.) This introduces the apostolic discourse, Matthew's second. We find a strong succession motif: Jesus is described as a shepherd, healer and teacher. However, he is moved with compassion at the sight of crowds he cannot reach. So he will appoint new shepherds to labor for God's coming harvest of people. The expression **like sheep without a shepherd** is from Numbers 27:16–17. There Moses, like Jesus, prays for a new shepherd (Joshua) to take his place as leader of Israel. The name of Joshua in the Greek version of the scriptures is "Jesus," thus making parallels stronger.

The Mission of the Twelve

10:5 (See Mark 6:7–13.) Jesus' injunction is unique to Matthew. **Go nowhere among the Gentiles and enter no town of the Samaritans, but go rather to the lost sheep of the house of Israel.** The mission of Jesus and his apostles during his earthly life was to their fellow Jews. This was the bible plan according to which the messiah was first for his own people and then, at the end of the world, for the Gentiles (Isaiah 2:1–4).

Jews regarded Samaritans as practically in the same category as Gentiles. This was because they were only partly Jewish, having broken the law to intermarry with Gentiles. As a result, there was considerable friction between Jews and Samaritans. The Jews did not allow them to help rebuild the first temple destroyed by the Babylonians about 587 B.C. The Samaritans retaliated by building their own place of worship. There exists a Samaritan community in Israel even to this day.

10:14 **Shake the dust from your feet.** This was a Jewish custom upon leaving Gentile territory. Here it is a sign of rejection. Sodom and Gomorrah were two towns destroyed by fire and earthquake in ancient times (Genesis 19:1–29) for their lack of hospitality and sexual abuse of strangers. They became a descriptive symbol of God's judgment on evil.

Coming Persecutions

10:16 (See Mark 13:9–13.) Unlike Mark's Gentile Roman persecutors, the context here is persecution from fellow Jews (10:6, 23). **A disciple is not above the teacher, nor a slave above the master.** However, such suffering is not a misfortune but an opportunity to identify with Jesus.

Courage Under Persecution

10:26 (See Mark 4:22.) Jesus' words are for everyone. Secrecy about his words now will come out on judgment day later. Matthew's gospel is the most severe in regard to future consequences and punishments.

Jesus, a Cause of Division

10:34 (See Luke 12:51–53.) A sword was a cutting instrument as well as a weapon. Jesus' message will not always have peaceful consequences, especially in a world where religious beliefs affected everything done at home or in business. Today, for example, we find much peaceful intermarriage, but in those days, religious practices entered into all of family life, especially food and meals. Therefore, heartrending family decisions had to be made.

Identification with Jesus

10:40 (See Mark 9:37.) The overwhelming emphasis is on the rewards of discipleship and identification with Jesus. It does not matter whether believers are apostles, prophets, teachers, holy men and women, or children. Those who receive them, receive Jesus and, through Jesus, God and his rewards. **Now when Jesus had finished instructing his twelve disciples…**This marks the literary end of Matthew's second discourse.

PATHWAYS TO FURTHER DISCOVERY:

What is meant by saying that Mark is more theocentric and kingdom-centered while Matthew is more Christological and community/church centered? Point to texts that illustrate this.

PERSONAL JOURNAL SUGGESTION:

The gospel stories are meant to place us into a "miraculous level of consciousness"—that of faith. Recall stories in your own life that seem "miraculous" in nature. Ask others if they have similar recollections. The results will be surprising.

The Messengers from the Baptist

11:2 (See Luke 7:18–28.) The questions and Jesus' answers show that Jesus was not the fiery messenger from God that the Baptist expected (3:11–12). In contrast, his compassionate mission is to the marginalized of society: the lepers, the deaf, the blind, the lame. His priority will be **The poor have the good news preached to them**.

Yet people made the long pilgrimage to John at the Jordan because he was the most honest and impressive prophet in history until the outbreak of God's kingdom. Instead of the previous ascetic and necessarily restrictive path of the Baptist, people are literally breaking down the doors of the kingdom of heaven.

11:16 Jesus, with his great sense of humor, contrasted old and new ways by an observation from children's games. Children, then as today, like to dress up, sing, imitate and sometimes make fun of adults' behavior at events such as weddings and funerals. While play-acting a wedding, some children played a flute for others to dance, yet not always with cooperation and success. The same was true about funerals. Jesus said the same was true about reactions to himself and the Baptist. **For John came neither eating nor drinking, and they say, "He has a demon."** The very same people see Jesus partying and associating with all kinds of people and say, **Look, a glutton and a drunkard, a friend of tax collectors and sinners**.

Thus some people are like changeable children in regard to wisdom.

Contrasting Responses to Jesus

11:20 (See Luke 10:13–16.) Here we find a striking contrast between the lack of response in prominent cities and the openness of little children in verse 25. Matthew carries the *child* motif even further than Mark. Jesus lifts his voice in characteristic spontaneous prayer/blessing: **I thank you Father, Lord of heaven and earth.** God hides his secrets from the so-called "wise and intelligent" of this world and reveals them to little ones. **Come to me, all you who are weary.** Jesus addresses the audience in the same way that Wisdom (a biblical personification of God) invites people to inner, deep knowledge (Proverbs 8–9). This contrasts with the external heavy burdens and obligations imposed by religion teachers the audience has known. Jesus' yoke is a gentle one based on imitation and love.

The Inner Meaning of the Sabbath

12:1 (See Mark 2:23–36.) These two stories illustrate the gentle yoke and easy burden of Jesus. Matthew adds, **something greater than the temple is here**—a hint that Jesus is greater than the temple and Jewish priesthood. **I desire mercy and not sacrifice** is a favorite Matthean scripture quote to reinforce Jesus' primacy of mercy over all religious rites (9:13 also). Our author omits the Markan reference (3:5) to Jesus' anger in the second sabbath story to better conform to the gentle image just presented and that in the next scripture of God's humble servant. In all, Matthew tones down the strong human emotions of Jesus that we saw in Mark.

The Humble and Gentle Servant of the Lord

12:15 The evangelist strengthens Jesus' "gentle and humble" image (11:29) by the biblical image of the gentle servant of the Lord in Isaiah 42:1–4. This servant does not push himself forward but works humbly and quietly. The double mention of Gentiles at the end hints at Jesus' future apostolate.

Jesus and the Ruler of Demons

12:22 (See Mark 3:20–30.) To answer the accusation that Jesus is a tool of Satan, Matthew adds the teaching on a tree and its fruits as a criterion. **On the day of judgment you will have to render an account**. It is so serious a matter to ascribe good actions to evil sources that such accusations will become a matter of final judgment.

The Sign of Jonah the Comic Prophet

12:38 (See Luke 11:29–32.) The comic prophet Jonah becomes the only outward sign that Jesus will provide. This Hebrew prophet was so shocked when asked to preach to foreigners in Assyria, traditional enemies, that he tried to avoid this mission by taking a ship in the opposite direction to Spain. A great storm came up and the sailors, at Jonah's request, threw him overboard when they learned what a terrible thing he had done. Yet God in his mercy sent a huge fish to swallow him, spit him up on shore and save him.

Of course this is comic literature whose meaning rather than details is important. Jonah then reluctantly preaches to the Assyrians that they have forty days left for repentance. To the great disappointment of Jonah, waiting for them to be destroyed, they sincerely repent and God spares them. Jonah is so upset by this that he cannot accept it and waits for the city to go up in smoke. Here I will not give you the unusual ending. Read the short book of Jonah and be surprised!

12:42 Another humorous story is the visit of the fabulous foreign **queen of the south** to see and hear the **wisdom of Solomon** (2 Kings 10:1–10). Another reference to Jesus as a wisdom teacher in Matthew who treasures this aspect of Jesus in this largest collection of his sayings.

Devils and Empty Houses

12:43 (See Luke 11:24–26.) The ancients believed that devils roamed around desert places until (like a virus) they could enter a willing host person. If exorcists, whether Christian or Jewish, merely cast out devils and leave the house (person) unoccupied, it only makes things worse. An opportunity has been lost to "remodel" the house. This introduces the next story where Jesus fills the house with his presence and teaching so evil spirits can no longer enter.

The True Family of Jesus

12:46 (See Mark 3:31–35.) Note the missing Markan opposition of Jesus' family. Matthew has already presented a beautiful image of mother and child in chapters 1 and 2 with which the story must harmonize. The contrasts here are much milder than in Mark. The family merely wants to speak to Jesus, not to demand that he come out. **Whoever does the will of my Father in heaven.** Mark has "will of God." The title from Matthew's Lord's prayer echoes often through this gospel.

PATHWAYS TO FURTHER DISCOVERY:

Can God "change his mind?" Read the short book of Jonah for an answer and apply it to Jesus' mission.

PERSONAL JOURNAL SUGGESTION:

What are the paradoxical messages in the comic book of Jonah? How can you apply it to your life story?

The Parable Collection, the Sower

13:1 (See Mark 4:1–20.) Chapter thirteen contains Matthew's third great discourse/collection on the parables of Jesus. In the introductory sower parable we have the words, "When anyone hears the word of the kingdom and **does not understand it.**" "Understanding" through deep reflection is a key word at the beginning and end of the parable and at the end of the collection with the question, **Have you understood all this?** (13:52).

The Problem of Weeds Among Wheat

13:24 Only in Matthew and a valuable key to a gospel theme. Often a parable has a humorous contrast to the ordinary human way of doing things. Any farmer or gardener would know that this advice is foolish concerning weeds and wheat: **Let both of them grow together until the harvest**. Yet God is indeed "foolish" in contrast to the usual human way of doing things. God's mercy toward everyone is a challenge to the audience's approach to others. It must be unlike the Pharisees who carefully screened all applicants concerning perfect religious observance.

It is also contrary to those who use deceptive approaches to conquering evil such as cruel punishment, massive imprisonment in more jails, racial cleansing, "elimination of undesirables" and similar means. The community/church approach must be like that of Jesus, leaving future judgment in God's hands. We find Matthew's strong descriptions of these rewards and punishments at the end of the parable and explanations (13:42–43; also, 13:49–50).

The Mustard Seed (see Mark 4:30)
A Woman's Secret Recipe

13:33 (See Luke 13:18–19.) Here a woman knows the secret of baking: just a small amount of yeast in several bushels of flour has such vitality that it can make dozens of loaves rise. Yet there is also another possible additional meaning. Yeast is also a symbol of corruption or evil since it can only be made by bread rotting and molding in darkness. God knows how to make use even of "evil" so the audience can always have hope.

Three Special Parables of Matthew

The parables of the hidden treasure and the pearl of great price are both special to Matthew. Each one features the *joyful finding*, which is the overwhelming grace of God, and *selling everything one has*, the total cheerful response as the cost of following Jesus. The fish net thrown into the sea is also proper to Matthew and continues the theme of "the good and the bad" of the weeds and wheat parable (see 5:45; 22:10). God's fishing net of grace goes out to all and gathers all kinds of fish, good and bad (and today, empty beer cans, etc.). The selection process takes place at the judgment.

Matthew's Special Insight and Conclusion

13:51 The parable collection concludes with the introductory words, **Every scribe that is trained for the kingdom of God**. The writer really describes himself as that scribe. In fact the Greek word, "trained" or "taught," used here is *matheteutheis* which looks like a play on the root of the author's own name or source. The special genius of Matthew as a gospel sage is to formulate a new synthesis of **what is new and what is old**. From his storehouse of memory he draws the "old," the Hebrew scriptures, and the "new," which are Jesus' words and teachings. **When Jesus had finished these parables**—this is a literary ending of Matthew's third great discourse.

Jesus Is Rejected in His Hometown

13:54 (See Mark 6:1–6.) With Matthew's emphasis on Jesus' person and power, he concludes, **he did not do many deeds of power there**. Thus he softens Mark's note that he could not do any deed of power (6:5).

PATHWAYS TO FURTHER DISCOVERY:

Trace Matthew's "mixed bag," good and evil theme through his gospel. Find illustrations of how Jesus himself applies it.

PERSONAL JOURNAL SUGGESTION:

Meditate on the parables of the treasure in the field and the pearl of great price and apply them to your own experience of finding God and responding to that call. What insights does this provide you?

The Martyrdom of John the Baptist

14:1 (See Mark 6:14–26.) Mark presented a more positive picture of Herod as desirous to save the Baptist as a holy man of God. Matthew modifies this to completely blame Herod as the responsible ruling authority. As in Mark, the Baptist's martyrdom prompts Jesus' withdrawal and the bread/banquet narratives so opposite to Herod's feast of death.

Jesus Feeds Five Thousand People

14:13 Matthew has omitted Mark's shepherd references, placing them instead as an introduction to the apostles' mission and succession to Jesus (9:36–38). This is a shift of emphasis to Jesus' words as the nourishing (shepherd) source and the apostles as transmitting them. Even in the loaves narratives, there is more emphasis on Jesus the teacher and his words as behind the meaning of bread. Matthew highlights Jesus' initiative, commands and actual words in the stories.

Jesus and Peter Walk on Water

14:22 (See Mark 6:45–52.) Mark presented Jesus' walking on water as overcoming the powers of death to provide a new meaning for bread. Only Matthew has Peter walking on water and conquering death also (see also 16:18). Peter's close association with the master is essential for the community and the meaning of the bread that nourishes them. The story is essentially a symbol of Peter's life story. He had protested that he could follow Jesus, relying on his own strength. But the heavy "Rock" began to sink under his own weight and deny three times that he even knew Jesus. Yet when he turned to Jesus in repentance, Jesus forgave him, took him by the hand, raised him up and "brought him back into the boat." The worship follows, **Truly you are the Son of God**. The messianic secret has disappeared in Matthew. Here all the disciples proclaim Jesus to be a majestic Son of God in power.

The Obstacles to Table Fellowship

15:1 (See Mark 7.) This is an introduction, like Mark, to prepare the way for the Canaanite woman and the second multiplication of bread, eventually for Gentiles. However, the obstacles of Jewish table fellowship traditions and foods stand in the way. Mark, for his Gentile audience, had concluded that Jesus declared all foods clean (7:20). Such a radical statement is not in Matthew, for his audience still keeps all the traditional teachings on foods and purification. Yet Jesus can say that **to eat with unwashed hands** (covered with Gentile dust) **does not defile**. This will be enough to allow at least a minimum association with Gentiles for the Jewish Christians in the audience.

The Foreign Woman Asks for Bread for the World

15:21 (See Mark 7:24–30.) This is much more detailed since it will be a real turning point for the audience, who will closely identify with the dialogue. This foreign woman addresses Jesus as Lord and messiah: **Have mercy on me, Lord, Son of David; my daughter is tormented by a demon**. Jesus does not even answer her, and the disciples appeal to the master to send away the troublesome woman. Then Jesus gives the reason he would not act: **I was sent only to the lost sheep of the house of Israel**. (See comments in Mark 10:5–6 on this statement as God's biblical plan.) The woman appeals a second time, now daring to come right up to Jesus, kneel at his feet and pray, Lord, help me. Still Jesus delays action, saying that the food of the children (Israel) is not for dogs (outsiders). The woman appeals a third time, humbly asking for crumbs of bread from the messianic table. Her faith overwhelms Jesus and he cures her daughter from a distance. Thus, Jesus symbolically reaches out to all Gentiles over space and time.

Jesus Heals the Marginalized and Handicapped

15:29 Another mountaintop scene is the setting and introduction for the second bread multiplication. Jesus welcomes a large audience of the handicapped **lame, the maimed, the blind, the mute and many others**. These represent the marginalized in society and prepare the way for those even outside the margins, the Gentiles, to eventually receive the messianic bread.

Jesus Feeds Four Thousand People

15:32 (See Mark 9:1–10.) In both multiplications, Matthew seems to have a less balanced diet, omitting specific mention of distributing the fish. His motive is to focus attention on the bread with its parallel in the last supper (26:26).

Demands for a Sign

16:1 (See Mark 8:11–13.) Matthew has more on this than Mark, specifying again **the sign of Jonah** as a comic sign. (See 12:38–42.) For the yeast of the Pharisees and Sadducees (6), see Mark 8:27–30.

Peter's Confession of Faith

16:13 (See Mark 8:27–30.) Peter's confession in Matthew is a central point in the gospel for which he has been paving the way. The confession of **messiah, Son of God** is a revelation and special privilege to Peter. It leads to Jesus' statement on Peter's future share of his power and his special role as a teaching successor: **You are Peter and on this rock I will build my church**. The word "church," *ekklesia* in Greek, occurs in the gospels only here and in 18:17. The scriptures use it to refer to the community of God's people Israel. **The gates of Hades will not prevail against it.** Hades or "Sheol" in Hebrew was the underworld, the place of the dead. Neither Jesus' death, nor that of Peter, will stop Jesus' continuity in this church.

I will give you the keys of the kingdom of heaven. Jesus promises to give his own teaching authority to Peter. "Keys" signify the power to include or exclude people from community membership. "Binding and loosing" means teaching authority and decisions. Whatever Peter does in this community role will be ratified by God in heaven. In 18:18, this will be confirmed regarding forgiveness and community membership. Tradition holds that Peter died in Rome in the early 60s A.D. This gospel was written at least twenty years afterward. This tells us that the author considered Peter's authority still active in those leaders who came after him.

Jesus Foretells His Suffering, Death and Resurrection

16:21 (See Mark 8:31–9:1.) Matthew focuses more attention on Peter's shock after hearing Jesus' prediction. Jesus replies that "Rocky" will be a stumbling stone to him. Like Mark, Matthew has three predictions of Jesus' death, each followed by instructions on following Jesus in the same way. Matthew, as usual, gives more attention to the return of the Son of Man as judge: **He will repay everyone for what he has done** (27). In Mark 9:1, the Son of Man was to come within the lifetime of the audience. Matthew however seems to have two comings, although he is not clear. One is in 16:27 as judge. The other (28) may be connected to the temple destruction (24:27) which had not yet occurred while Jesus was alive.

PATHWAYS TO FURTHER DISCOVERY:

Matthew has been called "the gospel for teachers." What are the teaching methods of Jesus that you observe in this gospel? Why was he so successful as a teacher?

PERSONAL JOURNAL SUGGESTION:

In life, we must follow the inner teacher, the Holy Spirit. Yet this Spirit often mediates through others—parents, teachers, friends, counselors. What is the best way for you to balance the inner teacher with the "outer" teachers?

The Transfiguration of Jesus,
17:1 (See Mark 9:2–13)

Jesus Cures a Possessed Boy

17:14 In Mark's parallel to the cure of the possessed boy, it is his father's faith that makes all things possible. This is omitted. Instead, Jesus takes the initiative to cure without the recipient's faith. When the disciples ask why they could not cure, Jesus' answer concerns the insufficiency of their faith as healers. Again we note Matthew's Christological emphasis.

Jesus Foretells a Second Time
His Death and Resurrection, 17:22
(See Mark 9:31–32)

Jesus and the Temple Tax

17:24 Every year there was a small tax on every Jew for the support of the temple, even after it was destroyed. Peter, representing authority, asks if Jewish Christians must pay this. In a humorous way, Jesus replies that they are not obliged but should do so to avoid giving offense. This illustrates the recommended attitude between the two groups: to recognize and respect each other, avoiding unnecessary disagreement even if they need a fantastic fishing miracle to do so!

Children as the Greatest in the Kingdom

18:1 The fourth great discourse in Matthew, the church or community instruction, begins at this point (18:1–19:1). (Chapter and verse numbers were added centuries after the gospel composition.) The discourse is introduced by the child theme that includes the little ones or lost ones in this chapter. **Unless you change and become like children.** The idea is to have the child's flexibility to change. This means new beginnings and repentance which will now be applied to various community situations. Other child sayings complete the child image and model. Temptation or abuse of these little ones is the most serious sin of all. They are so important that **their angels continually see the face of my Father in heaven**. Only Matthew has this traditional Jewish teaching on *guardian angels*, found especially in the book of Tobit.

Special Care for Lost Little Ones

18:10 The first example of lost little ones is found in the lost sheep parable. It really illustrates Jesus' own approach: to go to the lost sheep of the tribe of Israel (10:6). First, the lost ones must be a real community priority as shown by a diligent **search** for someone who is lost or has left the community. Then follows the joyful community celebration when someone is found and welcomed back into the community. **It is not the will of your Father in heaven that one of these little ones be lost.** The community search embodies God's own concern; the finding is God's own finding. This echoes again the sacrament of reconciliation.

Helping and Forgiving Lost Brothers and Sisters

18:15 The situation is this: someone attending community worship gatherings has seriously and publicly offended another member. However the person goes on unrepentant as if nothing has happened. This is a dangerous matter because every Christian is a repentant sinner by definition, saved now from future judgment by honesty and truth. Without this, God's future judgment awaits, especially for a hypocrite. The way to approach such a person is with great gentleness, sensitivity and secrecy (at first) with a humble, helping attitude: **Go and point out the fault when the two of you are alone.**

Only if this does not succeed should stronger means be taken—a small private group of two or three witnesses. If this fails, then as a final desperate resort: **tell it to the church.** If this is in vain, **only then let such a one be to you as a Gentile and a tax collector.** These are typical Jewish expressions for someone excluded from community meetings. The intention is medicinal, not punitive—temporary exclusion from community privileges so he or she can realize the harm done, and then return in repentance to be joyfully received back into the community as the lost sheep in the above parable. This is the root of the sacrament of reconciliation in its original community atmosphere.

Whatever you bind on earth will be bound in heaven. The church community's forgiveness is ratified by God in heaven. The concluding sayings show that this is because of Jesus' presence and power in the church. The word "church" is only found in 18:17 and in 16:18 concerning Peter's role as teacher.

The triple approach in this story—individual, two or three witnesses, then the whole community—was also used by the Jewish community of "monks" that lived a monastic-type life at

Qumran near the Dead Sea. This shows that Jesus' teaching in Matthew was also familiar in Jewish circles close to the time that he lived.

What About Forgiveness for Continual Backsliders?

18:21 The next group comprises continual backsliders. Just how far can a community go in forgiving those who are continually falling and then trying to come back? This is the humorous question of Peter, representing church authority's worries about this matter: **How often should I forgive? As many as seven times?** Peter thought he was doing very well. The number seven symbolizes a full and appropriate amount. However, God's forgiveness is foolish and extravagant by human standards: **seventy times seven times**.

The illustrative parable is really the Lord's prayer petition in story form: **forgive us our debts as we also have forgiven our debtors. The ten thousand talents**, representing debts to God, is so enormous that it would have taken a hundred reincarnations or more to pay off. **Yet, out of pity for him, the lord of the slave released him and forgave him the debt.** The word "forgive" is from the Greek root *charis*, and thus is an action of favor, grace and love.

The debt of a fellow servant to this man was infinitesimal in comparison, yet he threw his friend into prison. The other slaves (community members) are deeply distressed by such action and report it to the king. The king then handed him over to the torturers (to find out where he had hidden his money), for he had been deceptive in saying he could not pay. The ending of the story and its emphasis on the **heart** illustrates the genuineness and sincerity that real forgiveness should have.

Jesus' Teaching on Divorce

19:1 (See Mark 10:1–12.) Only Matthew has the famous exception clause concerning divorce **except for unchastity** (here and in 5:31). This shows that the author does not understand Jesus' statement in legalistic terms, but in reference to context and meaning. In view of his own Jewish background, the author considers unfaithfulness in marriage so unacceptable that it would break the bond of marriage and practically obligate a person to divorce. The story of Joseph and Mary suggests this in 1:19. Only the message of an angel kept Joseph from divorcing Mary for becoming mysteriously pregnant while under marriage contract.

Matthew's instruction is much more obviously a male-dominated affair. Four times he repeats that it is a matter of husbands divorcing their wives (19:3, 7, 8, 9), not allowing, as does Mark 10:12, the possibility for a woman to do likewise. Along with this, Matthew's gospel is more male-dominated than any of the other three.

Only Matthew has Jesus' statements on continence. This could apply to the above statements on divorced people not remarrying. However, it may be Jesus' exception to the biblical injunction that men and women should marry and bear children (Genesis 1:28). Jesus speaks of those who have the gift of continence in view of total service of the kingdom of God.

Jesus Blesses Little Children, 17:13
(See Mark 10:13–16)

The Rich Young Man

19:16 (See Mark 10:17–31.) In Jesus' answer to Peter's question, only Matthew has Peter and the twelve associated with the Son of Man in judgment even over Israel. Another emphasis on the new leadership of Peter and the twelve.

PATHWAYS TO FURTHER DISCOVERY:

Trace the theme of children/little ones, God's great reversal, as it goes through Matthew's gospel. How does this illustrate the approach of Jesus?

PERSONAL JOURNAL SUGGESTION:

If children have priority in the kingdom of heaven, what differences could this make in your own life and society around you?

Just Wages in God's Vineyard

20:1 Proper to Matthew. At first reading, the parable offends ordinary standards: part-time workers (some working only one hour!) are given preference and pay equal to those who work in the hot sun from dawn to dusk. Naturally those hard workers complain; why shouldn't they? Again, God's ways are foolish to poor human beings who only see part of the picture. The Merciful One knows that each man would need a full day's wage to buy food for the family: **Are you envious because I am generous?** But the complainers are stuck on the equal work, equal pay concept. God continually reverses human standards, so the introduction and the end of the parable have the same words: **The first will be last and the last first**. Matthew is thinking of the audience latecomers—the lost sheep, the poor, the disabled, and finally God's lost children, the Gentiles. These people found it a joyful privilege to work in God's vineyard and did not ask for an ironclad contract before starting to work.

Jesus' Third Prediction of His Death and Resurrection and the Request of James and John

20:17 (See Mark 10:32–45.) We smile to ourselves as Matthew has James and John make this ambitious request through their mother rather than directly themselves (as in Mark). Thus, the author shields James and John in the higher echelon authority levels of the twelve. But how does this make women readers feel?

Jesus Heals Two Blind Men

20:29 Again, two blind men to one in Mark 11:46–52. Thus, we have a *choral* emphasis to bring out audience participation. We have a triple acclamation using the Greek *Kyrie, eleison* (Lord, have mercy), a favorite powerful church mantra for nearly two thousand years. As they listen, the audience knows how blind they are to the deep meaning of Jesus' final entry to Jerusalem. Therefore they pray that their eyes may be opened so they can follow Jesus on the way.

Jesus' Triumphal Entry into Jerusalem

21:1 As in the above heading, Matthew has a triumphant entry in comparison with the limited teaching sign in Mark 11:15–19. Matthew's description better lends itself to liturgical celebration. Matthew explicitly quotes the underlying scriptures of Mark's account. It is a **very large crowd** that spreads their cloaks before him and **crowds** that go ahead of him shouting and singing **Hosanna to the Son of David!** This last messianic title is a secret in Mark but much more open in Matthew. The triumphant entry of Jesus shakes up the whole city (10). In Mark, Jesus more quietly enters the city, visits the temple area and returns the next day for the cleansing. Matthew designs his story for continued audience participation so they can annually celebrate "Palm Sunday" (the palms are from John's story) and sing the Hosanna acclamations.

Jesus Cleanses the Temple

21:12 Jesus' entry into the temple and the cleansing of the temple area is more like a triumphant messianic entry in Matthew. Jesus drives out *all* buyers and sellers from the vast temple open space. Mark's emphasis on the temple for the whole world (11:17) disappears along with the priests' reaction to Jesus' statement about the Gentiles' inclusion. Instead, the priests are disturbed about Jesus' reception by the little ones and the outcasts. The outcasts are **the blind and the lame,** usually excluded, whom Jesus heals in the temple. Matthew's children motif emerges again as the little ones (see 11:25–26) recognize Jesus as the Son of David while the "wise" chief priests and scribes are unable to do so. Matthew has omitted the Gentiles' place in the story, but the children and outcasts prepare the way for this.

Jesus Curses the Fig Tree

In Mark 11:12–14, the barren fig tree symbolically prepared the way for the future fruitful world temple. However, much of the symbolism is lost in Matthew as Jesus "zaps" the fig tree as a miracle to confirm his power regarding the temple.

The Authority of Jesus and the Parable of Two Sons

On the authority of Jesus see Mark 11:27–33. Only Matthew has the delightful reversal parable of the two sons. A child who says at first "no" is better off than one who says "yes" but does not come through. This was evident in the experience of John the Baptist. Prostitutes and tax collectors came to him at the Jordan and repented, whereas righteous religion teachers did not. Here, only Matthew notes that there were women among the crowds that came to the Baptist at the Jordan River.

The Parable of the Wicked Tenants
(See Mark 12:1–12)

The Parable of the Wedding Banquet

22:1 (See Luke 14:15–24.) An invitation from a king (representing God) to a wedding for his son is an extraordinary, once-in-a-lifetime privilege. It would be a supreme affront to neglect it. Prophets, messengers of God and finally Jesus have carried such invitations to people including the gospel audience. Yet history tells us that prophets to any country or people have rarely received an enthusiastic reception from a majority resistant to change. An interesting proverb runs thus: "People do not change their mind when they have no mind to change." It is unfair to single out the people of Israel.

The consequences of rejecting God's repeated loving invitation are serious: **The king was enraged. He sent his troops, destroyed those murderers, and burned their city**. It has often been stated that this refers to the Jewish war with Rome, 66–71 A.D. and the Jewish temple's destruction as a punishment for not receiving Jesus as messiah. This is simply not true, whatever the source of such an interpretation might be. It was actually a small minority of Jewish zealots and revolutionaries who provoked the war with Rome. However it can be said that the message of prophets to any country or people is usually peaceful and non-violent. Failure to receive such messages usually leads to the horrible consequences of war and suffering.

God, however, does not become discouraged by this response, but to the contrary even extends his invitation to more people: **Go therefore into the main streets and invite everyone you find to the wedding banquet**. God's purpose in his unlimited generosity is to fill his heavenly banquet hall with guests.

A second short parable is attached. God's loving invitation now goes to everyone, **good and bad** (a Matthean theme). Yet the responsibility remains to be fully clothed (in good works) for such a wonderful occasion. **For many are called but few are chosen.** This is not a numeric indicator, but one of choice and responsibility, which many are not willing to take.

On **Paying Taxes to the Government**, 22:15, see Mark 12:13–17. On the **Question of the Resurrection**, see Mark 12:18–27. On the **Greatest Commandment**, see Mark 12:28–34. Matthew adds that the second commandment to "love your neighbor as yourself" **is like** the first. They sum up all of God's teaching: **On these two commandments hang all the law and the prophets**.

A Final Response to the Scribes and Pharisees

23:1 (See Mark 12:38–40.) Mark has only two verses to conclude Jesus' teaching and make the transition to Jesus' last testament and farewell. In contrast, Matthew has a long scathing condemnation of the audience's former teachers among the Pharisees. This is a final plea not to turn back to them. Matthew has really put together a collection of Jesus' sayings, many in the literary form of seven woes and condemnations (13–37). Most of the sayings were originally from person-to-person controversy and clothed in the typical tough prophetic language used in the scriptures. Jesus even used such language in shaking up his own disciples.

However, it is hard to imagine that Jesus delivered such a severe discourse, word for word. Mark is more discreet and never has Jesus call Pharisees "hypocrites." The atmosphere is certainly unlike the beautiful loving and forgiving statements of the sermon on the mount. We can only suggest that Matthew, a persecuted Jewish convert, assembled the discourse. In doing so he did not reach the heights of the sermon on the mount and the master's own teaching.

Yet Matthew has in mind some of his audience who are *Christian Pharisees.* The Acts of the Apostles describes the stern attitudes of this group in the early church (15:1–5). Jesus ridicules their weakness for special titles and ostentation in 23:1–12.

The last part of the discourse (29–39) deals with the theme of response to prophetic challenges and can be applied to any age. We often honor prophets after their death by naming streets and parks after them. While they are alive, relatively few people listen to them. Many prophets have suffered and died as the result of bitter opposition. Jesus experienced the same lot. Yet his response is not anger but sorrow and care: **Jerusalem. Jerusalem, the city that kills the prophets...how often have I desired to gather your children together!** Like other prophets before him, Jesus says that the temple is no guarantee of God's presence and protection. **You will not see me again** (until you welcome me) are the farewell words of a prophet to his people.

The Destruction of the Temple and the End of the Age

24:1 (See Mark 13:1–37.) Matthew's fifth and last collection (chapters 24–25) is often called his eschatological discourse. It is Jesus' last will and testament for the future. The disciples ask, **What will be the sign of your coming and the end of the age?** The author puts together the end time with Jesus' second coming (*parousia*). Unlike Mark, Matthew's gospel has a view of extended time before this happens: it asserts **that the love of many will grow cold.** In Mark, the disciples' persecution will lead to a witness to the world and hasten the end. In Matthew, the persecution element is much briefer and not as prominent. Instead, patient endurance will prepare for the end time: **the one who endures to the end will be saved.**

In Mark, the destruction of the temple was a fore-shadowing of the return of Jesus but not to be confused with it. In comparison, Matthew appears to have two comings of the Son of Man. The first affects the temple in the concluding 24:27–28; the second is the universal coming for the world in verses 29–31. In this way Matthew can still retain Jesus' statement that some will be alive at the return of the Son of Man (16:28; 24:34).

Watchfulness—The Unknown Day or Hour

24:45 (See Mark 13:32–37.) Matthew adds the story of Noah's ark to bring out the element of suddenness and universality in the coming of the Son of Man. The expressions **two (men) in the field** and **two women will be grinding meal** depict universality for all men and women in typical proverbial form.

The parable of the faithful and unfaithful servants shows why some will not be ready. The wicked servant says to himself, **My master is delayed**. This hints that Matthew deals with the problem of Jesus' delayed return. Despite this, Jesus will surely return at an unexpected moment to render judgment on readers who have neglected to prepare.

The Parable of the Ten Bridesmaids

25:1 Only in Matthew, and the first of three parables to deal with the extended time before the master's return. Here again, **the bridegroom was delayed**. An old English translation captures some of Matthew's humor and keeps us from hanging on to some details as factual, rather than having deeper meaning. That translation described ten virgins, "five of whom were wise and five dizzy." The "dizzy virgins" foolishly neglected to bring extra oil for their wedding torches that could only last a short time. And of course no one else could give them, nor could they buy anywhere, the needed oil (of good words).

While they dilly-dally in this dilemma, the bridegroom comes and the "dizzy virgins" frantically knock at the banquet hall to get in, shouting, **Lord, Lord, open the door for us**. "Lord, Lord" is an address of prayer in Matthew. The women must have been Christian bridesmaids. But they are shocked to hear the groom's voice shout from inside, **I do not know you—** especially when they claim to know him so well. We have heard that expression before in the sermon on the mount. There Jesus stated that prayer, charismatic gifts and even miracles were not enough to identify someone as his follower (7:21–22).

The Parable of the Talents

25:14 After a long time, the master of the slaves came and settled accounts. Another hint of time delay for Jesus' return. What is to be done meanwhile? Again we find humorous exaggeration. The five talents was an enormous sum of money. Even in those days, "talent" had a double meaning in regard to someone's special personal gift or "talent." The "investment" of that talent involves the supreme meaning of life. It results in immense rewards in sharing the master's joy in the kingdom of heaven.

The "poor guy" who received only one talent still had a special gift. But like the "dizzy virgins" in the last story, he "buried his talent" and had nothing to show for the talent given him for good investment. The motto of the story is, **For all those who have, more will be given**. According to the biblical view, God's gifts, when given away and invested for the kingdom of heaven, keep multiplying in miraculous "geometric progression." It is something like the penny which, doubled each day for a month, becomes over a million dollars. As for those who guard their talent only for selfish use, it dwindles in value until it becomes almost useless or nothing—if we understand the humorous exaggerations that conclude the story.

The Judgment of the World

25:31 This concludes Jesus' teaching in a summary manner before the passion account. Centuries of artistic renderings of this scene keep us from appreciating the story element, the biblical background and even the paradoxical humor. It is hard to even imagine all the beautiful descriptions of God's love in this gospel (greater than all fathers and mothers in 7:11) ending in only a harsh judgment scene. A sense of perspective is needed. The very first words about Jesus in the gospel concern the meaning of his name, that he would "save the people from their sins" (in judgment). Before Jesus' birth, there were Jewish teachings (as well as in other religions) about heaven and hell. He certainly did not come down to earth and die on the cross to only teach something that was already known. In fact, the final words about eternal life and punishment are also found in Daniel 12, written centuries before.

The story elements need to be carefully examined. We find a careful weaving together of biblical texts, not a blow-by-blow description of a fearful judgment scene. The separation of sheep from goats comes from Ezekiel 34 where the main point is the shepherd's care (representing God) and protection of the sheep. On close examination, we find a humorous surprise element in the account: the just (the sheep) hear that there is really no judgment for them; it has *already* taken place: **Come, you that are blessed by my Father, inherit the kingdom prepared for you**. Then Jesus explains that the judgment already took place in their kindness and sensitivity toward people in their ordinary needs of daily life: **I was hungry and you gave me food, I was thirsty and you gave me something to drink**. This is the "orthopraxis" of the sermon on the mount where no "Christian works" such as miracles or charismatic gifts help at judgment (7:21–23; also 25:12).

As for the "goats" on the left hand, they hear the frightful words, **You that are accursed, depart from me into the eternal fire**. But again, they too are surprised because their judgment already took place long ago in their lack of sensitivity for the suffering: the hungry, thirsty, strangers, sick, naked or those in prison. *This memory and lack of sensitivity is already hell.* Their question to Jesus could be expressed, "What did we ever do to you, Lord, to deserve this?" The answer is the central gospel teaching about Jesus' identification with the poor, unfortunate and marginalized: **Just as you did not do it to one of the least of these, you did not do it to me** (45). The long repetitions in this story are not only memory aids but underline its importance as the concluding words of Jesus before the passion story.

PATHWAYS TO FURTHER DISCOVERY:

Discover how Matthew brings in the identification theme of this chapter as a central motif that goes through the gospel.

"Stepping into another's shoes" by imagining how he or she feels in a situation is a valuable path to new insights. Try this approach at the end of each day in regard to some trying person or situation.

The Plot To Kill Jesus

26:1 (See Mark 14:1–9.) The words, **When Jesus had finished saying all these things**, are a literary conclusion to Jesus' final discourse in Matthew.

Judas Agrees to Betray Jesus

26:14 (See Mark 14:10–11.) The contrast to Jesus' priestly covenant meal becomes stronger in Matthew as Judas does the opposite by making a covenant with the chief priests to betray Jesus.

The Passover with the Disciples

26:17 (See Mark 14:12–21.) Matthew's story highlights Jesus' provision and preparation of everything for this last supper. All must be according to his plans so the audience can know that when they celebrate a liturgy it is in accord with Jesus' plans and under his power: the Lord's supper. The dark shadow of Judas is most evident in Matthew: Jesus even identifies him and shows he is aware of his intentions (and those of the audience). Judas thus becomes the archetype of those who really do not make it a covenant meal in identifying with Jesus. Instead they have other conflicting interests.

The Institution of the Lord's Supper

26:26 (See Mark 14:22–25.) The following are the highlights of Matthew's version: He focuses more on Jesus' actual words and commands, whereas Mark described more non-verbal actions and symbolism. For example, regarding the cup, Jesus will say, **Drink from it, all of you**, whereas Mark will describe the action. In Matthew, Jesus' words are central as carrying present power and are easily repeated. Thus Matthew's account is more suitable as an actual liturgy—which through the centuries has followed Matthew closely.

This account also, concerning the cup, adds the words, **for the forgiveness of sin** (see commentary on Matthew 3:1–12). The author wishes to make a strong connection between Jesus' sacrificial shedding of blood and this forgiveness. Jesus becomes a new priest giving his blood for the forgiveness of sins. This compares with the high priest negotiating forgiveness from God by sprinkling blood on the ark of the covenant (Leviticus 16:32–34).

Peter's Denial
(See Mark 14:12–21)

Jesus Prays in Gethsemane

26:36 (See Mark 14:32–42.) Mark's story was an agonizing human struggle. On the one hand Jesus asked to have the cup of suffering taken away; on the other hand, he prayed to do his Father's will. Matthew tries to achieve a balance with the rendering, **If it is possible, let this cup pass from me; yet not what I want but what you want**. Jesus' grief seems more centered on his wavering weak disciples (in the audience as well), especially on Peter and Judas who are about to betray him. Jesus' request for audience participation is more Christological than Mark's: "Stay awake **with me**."

The audience also learns that their own "Lord's prayer" (6:1–13) is the very same prayer as that of Jesus in the garden with the identical Greek words, "Father," "Your will be done," and "Do not bring us into trial" (14, 39, 42).

The Betrayal and Arrest of Jesus

26:47 (See Mark 14:43–51.) We find much more interplay between Judas and Jesus at the last supper and here. Perhaps this is a hint that the constant initiative of Jesus and the image of the loving master finally triumphed at the end as it did with Peter. Jesus gently addresses Judas, **Friend, do what you are here to do**.

Only Matthew has Jesus explicitly stop the attempt to violently resist his arrest followed by the non-violent teaching: **All those who take the sword will perish by the sword**. Jesus then states that he could have asked for and obtained divine power at this point but chose not to. Thus, Jesus puts into practice his own teachings on non-violence in the sermon on the mount. Matthew has nothing on Mark's young man who fled away naked because this would not fit into the longer conclusion of his gospel.

Jesus Before the High Priest and Council
(See Mark 15:53–72)

The Suicide of Judas

27:3 The description of Judas' suicide is only in Matthew (but see Acts 1:16–18). Actually his failure was no worse than Peter's. However, in remorse he went to the chief priests for a forgiveness they could not give instead of going (as Peter did) to Jesus. Judas returned the blood money which the priests now had scruples about accepting. However, they decided to use it to buy a burial field for strangers. The purchase was significant and suggests that Judas' death was not in vain. In fact, in a mysterious way, it was a shadow of Jesus' death which would open the way for strangers to be believers. Thus Matthew seems to suggest that all was not lost for Judas despite his tragic end. Matthew also notes a fulfillment of scripture to indicate God's plan at work. This confirms a gospel teaching that God works even through what is considered human failure.

There is an air of mystery about Judas' death, which none of the other gospels mention. There are few suicides in the bible and only one other by hanging. This was the death of Ahithophel, a close friend and counselor of David the king and ancestor of Jesus (2 Samuel 16:15–17:23). This man betrayed

David, and after he was discovered, he went out and hanged himself. Given the different account in Acts 1:16–18 and the unusual concurrence with someone connected with David, we may ask if Matthew's intention is more to convey the meaning of Judas' betrayal rather than the suicide description.

Jesus Before Pilate

27:1,11 (See Mark 15:1–15.) On the important matter of responsibility for Jesus' death, see the comments on the above passage in Mark. Matthew adds here the divine intervention for justice through a dream to a Gentile, Pilate's wife. This parallels the gospel beginning and God's revelation to the strangers, the wise men from the east (2:1, 12). There is also a striking contrast between this foreign woman's concern for justice and the rulers in the next verse.

Pilate Sentences Jesus to Death

27:24 **So when Pilate saw that he could do nothing.** Matthew has Pilate appear almost a helpless victim of pressure. Strangely enough, Pilate performs a Jewish rite (Deuteronomy 21:6–8) in washing his hands in public to protest his innocence of responsibility for Jesus' death. This makes us wonder whether Matthew's scriptural interests have prompted this description. **Then the people answered, "His blood be on us and on our children."**

Matthew's above description creates grave difficulties. How can "all the people" make such a statement of responsibility if they are not there except for the limited "crowd" instigated by the rulers (27:20)? Also, Matthew had earlier stated that Jesus had to be arrested secretly for fear of opposition from the people (26:4–5). The other gospels have no statement similar to Matthew's. Unfortunately, the interpretation that the above words fasten responsibility on the Jewish people rather than on Pilate and his puppet authorities has occasioned untold suffering for millions of Jews through the centuries. This cannot be according to the spirit of Jesus' sermon on the mount.

The Soldiers Mock Jesus
(See Mark 15:16–20)

The Crucifixion of Jesus

27:32 (See Mark 15:21–32.) As in Mark, the last temptation of Christ is highlighted. However, Matthew draws a close parallel to Jesus' temptation in the desert, opening with the words, **If you are God's Son** (4:3, 6). Jesus is taunted as a powerless messiah who cannot save himself, let alone others, by coming down from the cross. This paradox prepares for what is to come: In an unexpected surprise, the powerful risen Son of God does "come down from the cross" to conquer death for himself and others.

The Death of Jesus

27:45 **At that moment.** Matthew adds a dramatic scene taking place when Jesus died: **The earth shook, and the rocks were split.** The earthquake is the "earth-shaking" opening of a new age through God's sudden intervention. Besides opening the temple veil (see commentary on Mark 15:38), the risen Jesus (his death and resurrection are put together) effects the resurrection of others also. The image is taken from the "passage of the bones" in Ezekiel 37. There God sends his Spirit to split the earth, open the graves and bring back his people from the "death" of the exile. In Jewish liturgy, that passage was read during Passover time and applied to the resurrection of the dead.

Now when the centurion and those with him...saw the earthquake and what took place, they were terrified. Note that Matthew's centurion is not alone as in Mark, but with others. So together, as a community response, they make the Son of God confession. In Mark, the emphasis had been on Jesus as obedient Son of God. But here the emphasis is on the earth-shaking power of the risen Son of God and its effect on the centurion and soldiers, signifying the Roman world.

The women have the same central place as in Mark, but we will see differences in the coming chapter.

The Burial of Jesus

(See Mark 15:42–47.) Matthew's account has Joseph of Arimathea as a disciple and not (as in Mark) a Jewish member of the council. The fact that he is **a rich man and laid it (Jesus' body) in his own tomb**, with the women watching, identifies the place exactly and shows that Jesus' body was not an unidentified part of a mass burial.

The Guard of Soldiers at the Tomb

27:62; 28:11 **This story is told among the Jews to this day** (28:15). "This day," noted by the author, was more than fifty years after the death of Jesus. Yet through the centuries, and even in recent times, there have been stories and claims that Jesus' body, only apparently dead, was taken down from the cross and revived by his disciples. Matthew, with tongue in cheek, responds to these claims by having an armed guard around the tomb, and ridiculing the testimony of soldiers who said that the disciples stole his body while they were sleeping!

The Resurrection of Jesus

28:1 (See Mark 16:1–8.) **Mary Magdalene and the other Mary went to see the tomb.** Mark had them come to anoint Jesus' body. But Matthew wants his audience to be better participants in the drama and accompany the holy women. There is another earthquake and a dazzling display of light and power as a divine messenger rolls back the great stone of death and opens the tomb. The angel also announces Jesus' resurrection, invites the women to see the tomb and gives them the commission, **Go quickly, tell his disciples.**

Jesus in this gospel directly appears to the women and repeats the angel's direction about his disciples' going to Galilee. In this way all the attention is focused on the final mountain scene as the climax of the gospel.

Conclusion and Commission of the Disciples

28:16 Now the eleven disciples went to Galilee, to the mountain to which Jesus had directed them. At the journey's end we climb the final mountain of enthronement and power toward which all the gospel mountain scenes have been moving. At the first mountain of temptation, Jesus was promised the world if he followed the devil's plans of power. By following God's plan of the cross instead, the risen Jesus now has **all authority in heaven and on earth**.

What follows is like a graduation ceremony. Jesus now transfers his divine authority to the eleven and commissions them to do what only he had been able to do: make new disciples: **Go therefore and make disciples of all the nations.** In the gospel, Jesus had limited their mission to the lost sheep of Israel (10:5–6). Now it is all-inclusive, to everyone, Jews and non-Jews; there are no more outsiders.

Baptizing them in the name of the Father and of the Son and of the Holy Spirit. This is already a baptism initiation ritual form based on the story of Jesus' baptism: the voice of the Father, the fellowship of Jesus with sinners, and the descent of the Holy Spirit. **Teaching them to obey (observe) everything I have commanded you.** These teachings are especially found in Matthew's five great discourses, above all the sermon on the mount. Jesus now hands them over to his disciples so they can be, like himself, "credentialed," empowered teachers for others.

And remember, I am with you always, to the end of the age. At the gospel beginning, Matthew announced that Jesus would be called **Emmanuel, which means "God is with us"** (1:23). Now Jesus fulfills these words for the future by announcing that the divine presence will always be with his disciples as they teach. The dynamic **word** of Jesus' teaching will be their **word** also, with all the presence and power of the master behind it. These words are addressed to the audience teachers whom Jesus has selected to continue and extend the apostles' divine commission. Jesus' words will continue to energize and empower them every time they listen to them anew in the gospel or teach others about them. Matthew's gospel is more than a teacher's manual. It is a live performance of the risen Jesus.

PATHWAYS TO FURTHER DISCOVERY:

In view of the last sentence above, look back on Matthew's gospel and list indications that he is trying to present his gospel as a "live performance."

PERSONAL JOURNAL SUGGESTION:

Study the meaning and context of the last supper in Matthew and identify with the people and events. Then note the best ways for you to fruitfully take part in a liturgy.

PART III
THE JESUS STORY:
THE VOICE OF LUKE

Introduction

(See comments below on Luke's own introduction 1:1–4.)

Prologue and Dedication to Theophilus

1:1 Luke is the only gospel with a personal introduction. Also, he is the only gospel writer with a double feature presentation. His second writing is the Acts of the Apostles where he refers immediately to his **first book**. Luke's concern is an account of **the events fulfilled among us**. This refers to the divine plan as shown in the biblical writings. Yet we will see that he is especially interested in showing that these scriptures have been fulfilled in a surprising and unexpected way that others have not presented adequately. This surprise will take the form of a gospel filled with many comic paradoxes, humorous stories and unusual occurrences.

Just as they were handed on to us by those who were eyewitnesses and servants of the word. Luke is at least a second generation Christian who uses existent sources. One of these is the gospel of Mark. Another source is what scholars call "Q," an abbreviation of the German word *Quelle*, meaning "source." This contains stories and materials that both Matthew and Luke have in common, but are not in Mark at all. We are not sure whether Luke used Matthew's gospel. We can estimate that

Luke wrote around the beginning of the second century A.D. A final source of Luke is the proper material only in this gospel. Luke has more special stories of his own than Matthew and Mark. These give us special insights into the character and motives of Luke as a gospel writer.

Luke's purpose is to write an orderly account for a certain *Theophilus*. This may be an actual person or it may be a way of addressing any sincere believer and listener to the gospel. We say this because the name Theophilus literally means "lover of God." Luke writes to him so **that you may know the truth concerning the things about which you have been instructed**. This **truth** may be to correct difficulties and misleading information of some Christian teachers. This truth also comprises special themes that Luke feels have not been sufficiently incorporated in previous writings. In addition, it includes his personal view of the gospel and that of the community from which he came. It would be difficult to outline all of this before even starting to read Luke. So we will point out these special Lukan features as we go through the gospel.

SUGGESTIONS FOR STUDY:

Start by reading the whole gospel in one or two sittings. As you read, note any special characteristics of this gospel that make it distinct from Matthew or Mark. Before you read any of the explanations, be sure to read the entire preceding gospel section.

The Gospel According to Luke

Announcement of the Birth of the Baptist

1:5 The first two chapters of Luke are often called a "mini-gospel." They summarize and foreshadow many great themes that Luke will develop in the rest of his gospel. As we pointed out in Matthew, birth stories of great heroes in antiquity often were told in view of the entire life of that hero. The first important group of stories in Luke concerns the annunciation and birth of John the Baptist. You will notice a section by section parallel between Jesus and the Baptist. This is because Luke is aware in his second volume, the Acts of the Apostles, that the Baptist, even after his death, had disciples scattered over the Roman world (Acts 18–19). Some of them knew very little about Jesus and naturally thought their founder was superior. Luke does not downplay the greatness of John, but tries to win over these disciples by showing how much greater Jesus is.

There were highly unusual circumstances surrounding the Baptist's birth. He came from the distinguished priestly tribe of Levi. His parents were like Abraham and Sarah—too old to hope for a child, yet they did not stop praying. The angel who comes to Zechariah is Gabriel, the same one who announced to Daniel about the coming new age of God (Daniel 9:17). **You shall have joy and gladness and many will rejoice at his birth.** This initiates the theme of joy and laughter in Luke; it is an echo of the birth of Isaac (meaning laughter) to Abraham and Sarah. Both of them had laughed when they heard they would have a child in their extreme old age (Genesis 17:17; 18:12, 21; 21:6).

He will be great in the sight of the Lord. He must never drink wine or strong drink. This refers to the Nazarite vow of consecration to God. Long, uncut hair was another obligation (Numbers 6:1–21). **Even before his birth he will be filled with the Holy Spirit.** Luke is the gospel of the Holy Spirit, whom Luke mentions more than Mark and Matthew together. Luke's second volume will show how this Spirit continues to work in the church.

All this news was simply overwhelming for the old priest. Just the idea of a child in his old age was stunning enough without the message that the child would be the long-awaited precursor to the messiah of the Jewish people. He was literally dumbfounded—speechless and shocked. The people outside the temple building were waiting for him to come out to give his priestly blessing. When he did come out, they realized he had seen a vision in the temple.

Announcement of the Birth of Jesus

1:26 Yet all the amazing news about the Baptist pales in comparison to that of Jesus' birth. In contrast to the prestigious priestly couple above, Mary is an unknown maiden from the little-known town of Nazareth. She was engaged (a marriage contract in those days) but had not yet gone to live with her husband. This would not happen for some time, only after a public wedding. Her husband's name is **Joseph of the house of David**. The mention of David is very important and will be repeated to show that Joseph will make possible the fulfillment of the biblical promises made to David about a future great king (2 Samuel 7:11).

He (Gabriel) said to her, "Greetings, favored one, the Lord is with you." Even today, the Greeks use the same word, *chaire*, meaning "rejoice" in their greetings. "Favored one" is from the Greek root *charis*, meaning grace, favor, or surprise. The English word "charismatic" comes from this root. Since the spiritual birth of every believer is a "virgin birth," the words, literally "Rejoice, favored one," are a greeting to each person in the audience. Luke will emphasize this grace or favor throughout his gospel.

Do not be afraid, Mary. Mary is so surprised by the preceding message that the angel has to assure her that she, Mary, is the one being addressed. **For you have found favor with God.** The word "favor," *charis*, is an explanation of the angel's greeting. It is also the new name and quality of every believer. **You will conceive in your womb and bear a son.** These words are really a quotation from Isaiah 7:14, which are about the birth of a future great son of David. They announce Mary's part in the great plan of God.

The Holy Spirit will come upon you and the power of the Most High will overshadow you. The words are similar to the description of God's coming to dwell in the completed tent dwelling for the ark of the covenant (Exodus 40:34). They suggest that Mary has indeed become a temple of God and is thus a model for the audience believers. **For nothing will be impossible with God** (from Genesis 18:14). As in the birth of Isaac in the Genesis text, faith concerns what is ordinarily considered impossible. Luke can be called "the gospel of the impossible."

Mary Visits Elizabeth

1:38 Continuing the joyful atmosphere, Mary hastens to go out and share the good news with her aged cousin Elizabeth. Since Mary has become like the ark of the covenant in bearing the promised child, her journey has a remarkable likeness to the biblical journey of the ark to Jerusalem in 2 Samuel 6:1–23. There, King David accompanied the ark on its journey, singing and dancing before it. During Mary's visit, Elizabeth tells her, **As soon as I heard the sound of your greeting, the child in my womb leaped for joy.** Elizabeth attaches special significance to this occurrence. The Greek word for "dance" is "jump," reminding us of the same word used of the musical David dancing before the ark. In addition, Mary stays three months with Elizabeth, just as the ark stayed three months in a certain house in the story of David. **Blessed is she who believed.** Here the writer, through Elizabeth, presents Mary as a faith model for believers.

It is very significant that Luke writes about Mary in such glowing terms even though it is many years after her death.

Indirectly, he tells the audience that if God, through an angel, calls Mary "blessed," and if the Holy Spirit does so through Elizabeth, then the community can do so too. They can also greet Mary, like the angel, with the words, "Hail, full of grace." Luke foretells this through the announcement of Mary, "All generations will call me blessed" (2:48).

Mary's Song of Praise

1:46 David first came to the court of Saul, the previous king, as a musician and singer. Luke takes up the messianic musical theme as no other gospel does. It has been called the "song and dance" gospel. Mary's joyful song announces some important gospel themes: **the lowliness of his (God's) servant**—the theme of humility; **he has filled the hungry with good things**—the gospel of bread for the hungry; **he has helped his servant Israel**—a deep appreciation for the Jewish roots of the believer.

The Birth and Naming of the Baptist

1:57 The surprises continue as Elizabeth, like Mary and other women in this "gospel of women," takes the initiative about John's name despite family objections. All of this finally shakes up the speechless Zechariah. He makes signs to request a writing tablet and puts down **His name is John**. Then his tongue is suddenly loosened to praise God in the coming prophecy and canticle.

The Song and Prophecy of Zechariah

1:67 A favorite theme of Luke is God's continual plan and guidance through history to make possible these unusual events. The newborn child will initiate the last stage of preparation for the world: **to go before the Lord to prepare his ways**. John's ministry will be like a new light of day bringing **the tender mercy of our God** on earth through a ministry of **forgiveness of sins**. For the first time, the Lukan theme of peace is sounded and will later resound through the gospel: "to guide our feet into **the way of peace.**" While peace summarizes all the messianic blessings, it will be a repeated refrain in this gospel especially regarding forgiveness and non-violence.

The Birth of Jesus

2:1 **In those days a decree went out from Caesar Augustus.** Luke likes to locate events in Jesus' life within the context of world history. This is to oppose the idea that Jesus could be a mythological figure like the founders of Rome or Greece. Yet he does so with a sense of humor. The Roman emperor Caesar Augustus thought he had the world in the palm of his hand as he made plans to register everyone for military and tax purposes. Yet in doing so he made possible the fulfillment of the scriptures regarding the birth at **Bethlehem** of a rival who would surpass him!

And she gave birth to her first-born son and wrapped him in bands of cloth. These bands of cloth (swaddling clothes) are mentioned here and in 2:12. All new-born babies by custom were so wrapped to keep their spine straight. Luke's purpose is more than descriptive. He wants to show that Jesus is completely human in every possible way, not just by resemblance. He does not drop down from heaven as in some myths, but is truly one of us. This is to counter some gnostic-oriented Christians who tended to regard the human body as a mere corruptible outer shell.

And laid him in a manger. The word "manger," a common feeding bin for animals, has special meaning for the audience. It is even repeated three times, the second time with the announcement: **This will be a sign for you**. The audience key to this sign lies in the very first words of the greatest prophet, Isaiah. God announces through him, **The ox knows its owner and the donkey its master's manger but Israel does not know, my people do not understand**. (Note the scriptural origin of the animals in the traditional crib scene.) The donkey is traditionally the dumbest of animals (or the smartest!). A donkey even talks and gives advice in Numbers 22:28. (All right, if you don't believe me, read the text for yourself!) Yet a donkey knows where to go to get food: to his master's manger. So the sign of the

manger tells the wise ones in the audience that the child Jesus in
the feeding place symbolizes that he is the source of bread for
those seeking true nourishment. Luke is a "gospel of bread." He
begins with this theme and ends on it also. This occurs when the
disciples traveling to Emmaus recognize Jesus in the breaking of
the bread (24:31).

Because there was no place for them in the inn. Another
Lukan theme, that of the homeless stranger. Salvation history
begins when Abraham and Sarah went out of their way to
generously provide hospitality for three traveling strangers
(Genesis 18:1–15). The gospel will end on the same theme, but
reversing the gospel beginning. A mysterious stranger, Jesus in
disguise, meets two disciples on the way to Emmaus and
converses with them. The disciples press the stranger to stay
with them at the place where they were going. As a result, they
recognize the risen Jesus in their midst as they break bread
together (24:29–31).

The Shepherds and the Angels

2:8 Luke's surprises continue. **There were shepherds
living in the fields, keeping watch over their flocks by night.**
Again the story is told in terms of scripture (1 Samuel 16:1–13).
There we find a Bethlehem scene when the prophet Samuel
seeks a new king for Israel. The prophet is invited to a special
banquet at the house of Jesse, where his seven sturdy young
sons are at table. Samuel feels sure that one of them will be the
next king, yet is disappointed that God does not want any of
them. Finally the prophet learns that there is another son, a
"little one" out in the fields tending sheep. Samuel calls for him
(David) and anoints him to be king over Israel.

With this scriptural background, the shepherds in the
Christmas story symbolize the "little ones" of the audience who
are waiting and watching. They are the ones, like children today,
who recognize the "little one" in the manger. Luke's emphasis
on children will continue throughout his gospel.

Good news of great joy to all the people. This expression
summarizes the whole joyful atmosphere of Luke's gospel. **A
savior who is Christ the Lord.** "Savior" and "Lord" are two

favorite titles in Luke. Since he has never seen Jesus in the flesh, he knows him as a risen majestic Lord and merciful savior. "Lord" is the title given to God in the Greek Old Testament in place of the revelation name "Yahweh," meaning "the one who is." "Lord" is also a title that the Roman emperor cherished as "lord and master" of the whole world.

Suddenly there was with the angel a multitude of the heavenly host, praising God. Here the joy moves to celestial circles as angels form a choir to sing God's praises. These praises and blessings will echo throughout Luke. **Peace on earth** is the angels' message. Continuing the theme of peace from 1:79, the celestial harmony and peace come down from heaven and spread.

The Circumcision and Naming of Jesus

2:21 Luke's Acts of the Apostles places great importance on the name of Jesus. Believers call on his name in prayer and even work miracles through it. A biblical name invokes the person's presence and power. Therefore, the gospel prepares for this by noting Jesus' circumcision, eight days after his birth, a time when names were given (1:59). It is a name with special meaning ("One who saves") because it was chosen not by his parents but by God (1:31). In Matthew's gospel, an angel spoke to Joseph and guided him through dreams. In Luke, God speaks to a woman and guides her. Few biblical women had this privilege; it was usually their sons or husbands.

Jesus Is Presented in the Temple

2:22 Following biblical law, forty days after the child's birth his parents presented him in the temple. This was an ancient ritual that every first-born son should be dedicated to God as a priest. However, this changed when the tribe of Levi took over the priesthood. After this, the ritual was altered so that parents "bought back" their son after presenting him for the priesthood. In Jesus' case the ritual was real because his parents dedicate him to God for temple service as a priest of God in a new sense. This will entail much suffering: Simon prophesied to Jesus' mother that as a prophet he will face much opposition and **a sword will pierce your (her) own heart.**

The highlight of Simeon's canticle is the prediction that the child will be **a light of revelation to the Gentiles and for glory to your people Israel.** Instead of the friction we saw in Matthew, Luke has a calmer, more peaceful appreciation of the Jewish roots of Jesus and his impact on his own people. The evangelist foresees that God's plan calls for a harmonious union of Jew and Gentile in the future.

Then an older woman, a prophetess, appears and begins to talk about the child to everyone. Luke has a keen appreciation of the charismatic gifts of the Spirit such as prophecy. His two volumes have many stories of dreams, revelations, healings and other gifts of the Spirit. Luke is anxious to show that the Spirit equally moves all people old and young, male and female, as well as people of different social classes. Our evangelist sees this as a fulfillment of the prophecy of Joel 3:28–29 which he quotes in Acts 1:17 as follows, **In the last days...I will pour out my Spirit upon all flesh, and your sons and daughters shall prophesy and your young men shall see visions, and your old men shall dream dreams. Even upon my slaves, both men and women, in those days I will pour out my Spirit.**

After Jesus' return to Nazareth, Luke notes, **The child grew and became strong, filled with wisdom; and the favor of God was upon him.** Here we see the biblical motif of wisdom applied to Jesus. This is also another important emphasis on Jesus' humanity, which we first saw in regard to the mention of swaddling clothes in 2:7. Jesus grows and matures like any other human child. This is repeated again when Jesus comes to his twelfth birthday (2:52).

The Boy Jesus Among the Temple Teachers

2:41 The twelfth birthday is unique for every Jewish child. It is the age they become a **bar mitzvah,** "son of the law," or **bat mizvah,** "daughter of the law," in many modern congregations. Twelve is the legal biblical age for assuming all the responsibilities of an adult. For Luke, it becomes an occasion to sum up Jesus' future vocation: he will become an extraordinary teacher, for his parents find him **in the temple sitting among the teachers**. However, this call means leaving his parents. The three-day loss and finding foreshadows the loss of his life and finding it again.

Naturally his mother asks him, **Child, why have you treated us like this? Your father and I have been searching for you in great anxiety**. In his reply, Jesus makes a sharp contrast with those words: **Did you not know that I must be about my Father's interests?** His parents did not understand this. The lack of understanding of Jesus' words and the scriptures is a repeated theme in Luke. God's plans are so surprising that only he can make them known. **Yet his mother treasured all these things in her heart** (see also 2:19). Mary becomes an audience model for those who ponder over Jesus' words and the scriptures to find meaning for their lives. This theme is from the prophet Daniel who also pondered when God gave him a special revelation about the future new age of God (7:28; 9:27).

PATHWAYS TO FURTHER DISCOVERY:

How do chapters 1 and 2 as a "mini-gospel" sum up some of the great themes that will go through Luke's gospel?

PERSONAL JOURNAL SUGGESTION:

Mary the mother of Jesus is the first Christian "journalist," although she wrote her thoughts in her heart rather than on paper (2:19, 51). It is not necessary to write a great deal in our journal, but it should always be a reminder, for our own eyes, of deeper matters going on in our hearts.

The Preaching of John the Baptist

3:1 **In the fifteenth year of Emperor Tiberius.** Again Luke the historian gives us times and dates. The story of John the Baptist is even found in the non-biblical accounts of Josephus, a Jewish historian of the first century. While Matthew and Mark have the same prophecy of Isaiah, only Luke continues, **And all flesh shall see the salvation of God**. This becomes almost a theme song for Luke's second volume, the Acts of the Apostles, which traces the spread of the gospel through the world.

The crowds asked him, "What then should we do?" Throughout Luke we find very practical directions for everyday life for the audience/readers. First, the basic needs of every human being are a priority: **Whoever has two coats must share with anyone who has none and whoever has food must do likewise.** Many people thought that conversion might require taking on a new job with less moral risk. However, the Baptist does not ask that even of soldiers and tax collectors who had the strongest temptations for injustice, extortion and violence.

Only in Luke and John 1:19–20 does the Baptist answer questions about whether he is the messiah. This shows how popular a figure he was. We will notice that John and Luke have many similarities.

The Baptism of Jesus

2:21 Unlike the other gospels, Luke does not describe Jesus' actual baptism. Instead he focuses on Jesus' prayer which prompts the coming of the Holy Spirit. This is a model for the community assembling to pray for the coming of the Spirit. This happens often in the Acts of the Apostles, especially at the first Pentecost (1:14). In Luke, Jesus stops to pray before many great important decisions in his life.

The Ancestors of Jesus

3:23 **Jesus was about thirty years old when he began his work.** We like precise details like this. But we begin to wonder when we read that David was thirty years old when he became king and Joseph was thirty when he became chancellor of Egypt. Is thirty a symbolic age for maturity and wisdom as it was for Jewish teachers?

Matthew provided a genealogy of Jesus as far as Abraham and Sarah, parents of the Hebrew people. However, Luke, with his universal emphasis, pushes it back to Adam and Eve, the parents of the whole human race. According to the biblical story, our first parents faced temptation and failed. Now Jesus faces temptation and must reverse this failure if he is to affect all people on earth. So the following temptations of Jesus have cosmic dimensions in Luke.

The Temptation of Jesus

4:1 (See Matthew 4:1–11.) Luke reverses Matthew's order of the three temptations to place the Jerusalem temptation last. This is to link the **throw yourself down** words to Jesus' last temptation on the cross. **When the devil had finished every test, he departed from him until an opportune time.** This statement, only in Luke, looks ahead to the passion story where we have Jesus' cosmic struggle with the powers of darkness. This will serve as a model for the audience in "Christian combat."

Jesus Is Rejected in His Home Town

4:16 Luke begins the story of Jesus' ministry with his sermon and rejection in his own hometown. This becomes the setting for an introductory tableau presenting the meaning of his whole mission. Jesus chooses Isaiah 61:1–2 to present the goals of his teaching: **The Spirit of the Lord is upon me...to bring good news to the poor...release to captives...to let the oppressed go free...to proclaim the year of the Lord's favor.** This last phrase refers to the great biblical jubilee year announced every fifty years by the blowing of trumpets (Leviticus 25:1–52). During that year, all property had to be returned to its original owners; slaves (through debts) had to be freed, and many debts were pardoned. The ideal behind it was that all land belonged to God and was only lent to us for temporary use and should be shared equally among all (Leviticus 25:32). The founders of our country knew that text well, for they inscribed the opening words on the Liberty Bell: **Proclaim liberty in the land** along with the biblical citation (Leviticus 25:10). However, as we have seen, the biblical text announced quite a different view of freedom. Jesus' message embraced the ideals of the jubilee year in his preaching of good news to the poor.

However Jesus' hometown wanted a spectacular miracle display rather than ethical challenges of justice. Jesus warns that prophets generally are rejected by family and friends but are received by strangers. He cites the example of the great Hebrew prophets Elijah and Elisha. The townspeople drive Jesus to the brink of the cliff at the end of town, perhaps to push him into some miraculous feat (like Jesus' third temptation). Jesus mysteriously escapes at this point because he must go on to Jerusalem and complete his prophetic work before his arrest and death.

The Man with the Unclean Spirit
(See Mark 1:21–28)

The Cures at Simon's Home

4:38 (See Mark 1:29–34.) **He laid his hands on each of them** and cured them (40). This personal and individual touch is noted by Luke. It may be influenced by his profession as a doctor. Paul refers to Luke as his "beloved physician" (Colossians 4:14).

Jesus Calls His First Disciples

5:1 Typical of Luke, he takes another important occasion and expands its meaning for every disciple called to be a **fisher**. Luke does this because of his "poetic license." The miraculous draught of fish is only found elsewhere in a post-resurrection apparition of the risen Jesus in John 21:1–8. However, since Luke only knows one risen Christ, he does not hesitate to combine it with the disciples' call in Matthew and Mark 1:16–20 that did not have this miracle. The focus is on the power of Jesus' **word** that now speaks through his disciples, in contrast to ordinary words and efforts.

After fishing all night with no results, the fishermen were frustrated and exhausted. Jesus challenges them to new fishing techniques under his directions. The disciples represented by Peter protest but finally say, **If you say so, I will let down the nets**. Simon Peter is the leader of the fishing expedition (church's mission) and has an important place in Luke. He is astonished at the extraordinary results and says, **Go away from me, Lord, for I am a sinful man**. For Luke, the response of any disciple must be immediate and total: **They left everything**. This totality is characteristic of Luke who will never describe half-measures when it comes to response to Jesus.

PATHWAYS TO FURTHER DISCOVERY:

Describe how Jesus' first sermon sums up his whole ministry as you read it in light of the whole gospel.

PERSONAL JOURNAL SUGGESTION:

How does the the apostles' call in 5:1–11 shed light on your own special calling and the best way to follow it?

Jesus Cleanses and Cures a Leper

5:12 (See Mark 1:40–45.) The closing reference to Jesus' habit of withdrawal for prayer is typical of Luke and introduces the central teaching on healing and forgiveness in the next story.

Jesus Heals and Forgives a Paralytic

5:17 (See Mark 2:1–12; Matthew 9:1–8.) Mark presented this important account about forgiveness of sin in the early church. Luke singles out the opening audience **of Pharisees and teachers of the law** who had come from even as far as Jerusalem to observe Jesus. This audience directs our attention to the central question of authority to forgive sin. Luke's crowd reacts, **We have seen strange things** (literally in Greek, *paradoxa*) **today!** The emphasis is on the unusual nature of Jesus' teaching in contrast to other official religion teachers.

Jesus Calls Levi the Tax Collector

5:17 (See Mark 2:13–17; Matthew 9:9–13.) Luke makes even more of this extraordinary application of Jesus' teaching on forgiveness. Levi is so responsive to Jesus' acceptance that he **left everything**. Then Levi not only has Jesus for dinner but gives a **great banquet** for his own associates as well. This is simply "too much" for the ever critical and observant "religion teachers." Luke adds the matter of **repentance** to Jesus' final statement that he has not come just to call righteous teachers but sinners. This is a Lukan emphasis on the complete change of life-style that should accompany forgiveness.

Fasting or Feasting in the Kingdom of God, 5:33
(See Mark 2:18–22)

Sabbath Questions, 6:1
(See Mark 2:23–3:6)

Jesus Chooses the Twelve

6:12 (See Mark 3:13–19.) **He went out to the mountain to pray.** This gospel of prayer notes Jesus' prayer before special decisions as an audience example. Luke also mentions that Jesus chose the twelve out of a larger group of disciples, so the audience would not feel excluded.

The Sermon on the Plain

6:17 (See Matthew 5–7.) Matthew's sermon on the mount had parallels to Moses giving the law to the Hebrew people from atop Mount Sinai. Luke's "sermon" comes down from the mountain to the plain of the world. Both evangelists draw from the same "Q" source (see introduction), but Luke omits all specific bible references such as "it was said to you, but I say to you." Luke's audience is mostly Greek Gentiles, and he presents Jesus' ethical teachings in a way that would surpass all they had learned in their education. The Greek schools emphasized the virtues, especially friendship, in their training. Jesus presents a new way that goes far beyond the reciprocal nature of friendship by describing a quality of love that asks for no return.

Like Matthew, the sermon opens with a series of blessings: **Blessed are you who are poor**. However Luke emphasizes the present social condition of those who, in his gospel, have less so that everyone will have enough. This will be illustrated in the Acts of the Apostles where early believers sell possessions and property to provide daily help and food for the needy (6:1–2; 2:43–44; 4:32–37). The "now" or present comes out explicitly in the next blessing: **Blessed are you who are hungry now.** Matthew, we saw, drew attention to the inner qualities by writing the first blessing regarding the **poor in spirit.** In Luke, Jesus does not praise poverty in itself but those who are poor as the result of voluntary sharing. Luke follows with a series of woes: **But woe to you who are rich.** In each case God will "reverse" those who will not reverse themselves.

Love your enemies. Matthew simply writes "to pray for them." But Luke has very concrete gestures: **do good to those who hate you, bless those who curse you.** This is meant to be a humorous reversal of the ill will of others. It is "ridiculous," a matter of laughter, because Luke sees this as only made possible by the extraordinary grace of God. Luke next goes to the source of such an "impossible" attitude. This comes from imitation of God, **for he is kind to the ungrateful and the wicked.** Luke does not have the exact words of Matthew but examines the underlying quality that is what we would call "unconditional love." He also interprets Matthew's, "Be perfect as your heavenly Father is perfect," by writing, **Be merciful as your Father is merciful.**

Reversing a Judgmental Attitude

6:37 (Matthew 7:1–20.) Luke completes Matthew by describing the reversal of a judgmental attitude. **Forgive and you will be forgiven; give and it shall be given to you.** Luke then describes a humorous superlative: Whatever we give comes back to us from God and others in surprising multiplication. This image contrasts that of a typical merchant using his long robe to measure out grain: a shrewd seller makes the amount seem as large as possible by keeping it loose and spread out; instead, God shakes it together, presses it down and has it overflowing over the edges.

Matthew and Luke end their "sermons" in the same way. Yet it is interesting to see how Luke adapts it to the climate and geography of his audience. Matthew had a man who built too close to a dry creek and thus vulnerable to flooding from sudden rain. Luke has a deep foundation on rock to guard against rising, swollen rivers. Thus both evangelists hand down the sense of Jesus' words, rather than a word by word version.

Jesus Heals a Centurion's Servant

7:1 (See Matthew 8:5–13.) The most unpopular men in Israel were Roman centurions. They were in charge of a rough army of occupation often guilty of extortion, violence and plundering (2:14). Yet Luke points out that there were good people, close to God, among hated foreigners. The centurion **loves our people** and even **built our synagogue**. Only Luke mentions that he went first to the Jewish elders, who interceded for him. This is a pattern we observe in the early church through the window of the Acts of the Apostles. There, missionaries go first to the synagogue, and thereby attract God-fearing Gentiles already drawn to Jewish monotheism and its ethical code. These Gentiles in turn tell others about the Christian message. Luke is anxious to present a positive picture of Judaism as a stepping stone to reaching the rest of the world.

Jesus Raises the Widow's Only Son

7:11 Found only in Luke, the story has a remarkable literary similarity to the biblical story of the widow's son raised to life by Elijah (1 Kings 17:17–24). The story illustrates Luke's view of Jesus as the risen Lord and master of life and death. This life-giving power reaches even to the most desperate human situation—that of the sudden death of young man, the **only son of his mother, a widow**.

Out of compassion, Jesus must take the initiative because deceased people cannot ask for themselves. In dramatic fashion, Luke describes the unstoppable procession of death leaving the town gate. Simultaneously, Jesus and his disciples are drawing near to the city. According to custom, he would be expected to turn back and join the funeral march toward the cemetery. Instead, Jesus stops the procession of death and brings the boy to life, after which the funeral cortege turns around to join Jesus and the procession of life re-entering the city. **Young man, I say to you, arise**. The powerful voice of Jesus reaches even to the dead and they respond! **The dead man sat up and began to speak.**

Messengers from John the Baptist

7:18 (See Matthew 11:2–19.) Luke and Matthew use the same "Q" source. However, in his love for paradox, Luke notes how prominent religion teachers stood by and watched at the Jordan River. In contrast, even sinners and tax collectors (29–30) entered the Jordan waters for forgiveness and the gift of God's grace.

The Pardon of the Repentant Woman

7:36 Only in Luke, but with similarities to the Bethany banquets in the other gospels at the beginning of the passion narrative. Immediately, the contrast in the story appears. The Pharisee is a fine respected leader. Anyone would be privileged to be invited to his house for dinner. On the other hand, a woman of doubtful reputation sneaks into the home and places herself by the feet of Jesus. The Pharisee of course would not even be seen near such a person; her entry into the house was like the desecration of a holy place. While women often performed the roles of hospitality, her gestures were unusually extravagant and affectionate. She used her own hair to dry Jesus' feet which she kissed many times. The good Pharisee of course was shocked.

He said to himself, **If this man were a prophet, he would have known who and what kind of a woman this is who is touching him**. The Pharisee immediately presumes that this woman is employing the seductive arts of her profession. Jesus, however, as a prophet, sees everything in reverse: Simon, his host, is the sinner and the disreputable woman is the holy person. Jesus illustrates this through a story of two debtors, one with a small sum, and the other, ten times larger. Jesus asked Simon which of the debtors would love most in return. Simon, of course, replies that it is the one with the larger debt.

The key to the story lies in the meaning of the Greek word, "forgive." It is from the Greek root *charis*, which means grace or favor. Forgiveness is an action of love, and the woman who experienced this responded in kind. Jesus then draws out the contrast between the two people. Jesus notes that Simon had not given him the usual signs of welcome through a washing of feet and hospitality. Something deeper seems implied: Simon did not really take Jesus' forgiving presence into his home because he felt he did not need it—he was already a holy and just man. In contrast, the woman supplied the kisses of welcome in a most affectionate way—she offered Jesus a welcome into the house of her inner self. Her great love is a sign she has already experienced forgiveness whereas the "holy" Pharisee did not know what the word even meant, for he had never felt he needed it. So Jesus concludes: **Her sins, which were many, have been forgiven; hence she has shown great love. The one to whom little is forgiven loves little**.

PATHWAYS TO FURTHER DISCOVERY:

Contrast the meaning of Luke's sermon on the plain (6:17–49) to views on life of various people you have met. How can a person move toward the apparently impossible high ideals expressed in the above passage?

PERSONAL JOURNAL SUGGESTION:

In a meditative way, go slowly through the story of the penitent woman in 7:36–50 while identifying with each character. What insights do you gain from this?

The Women Who Travel with Jesus

8:1 Only Luke specifically names the women following Jesus on his journeys. This close association with women would be another unexpected surprise to the male-dominated religion of Jesus' time as well as to the gospel audience. In addition, some of these women had been cured of illnesses that must have made them seem "unstable" to many people—for example, **Mary called Magdalene from whom seven demons had gone out**. We cannot derive too much from this description. Perhaps it was a way of saying that she was at least a very lively character in her day! Luke also notes that some women had considerable means at their disposition, and perhaps a good amount of independence. In his second volume, Luke will note the important contribution of women who had considerable means and independence. For example, Lydia of Philippi was a prominent business woman at the head of a large household (Acts 16:14–15).

The Parable of the Sower

8:4 (See Matthew 13:1–23.) In this parable, Luke emphasizes the quality of the **heart** in those who really listen (the good ground). Also, **they bear fruit with patient endurance** (15). Patience and endurance are special Lukan themes.

The Lamp Under the Jar, 8:16
(See Mark 4:21–25)

The True Family of Jesus

8:19 (See Mark 3:31–35.) There is a remarkable difference in this story about Jesus' family when compared with Mark. The family does not demand that Jesus come out of the house but only **could not reach him**. Also, there is no sharp contrast between Jesus' disciples and the family. Luke's version differs because of the exalted view he has of Jesus' mother that we saw in the first two chapters. Also, in the Acts of the Apostles, the mother of Jesus and the family are prominent in the Jerusalem community as they pray and await the coming of the Holy Spirit (Acts 1:14).

Jesus Calms a Storm, 8:22
(See Mark 4:35–41)

Jesus Heals the Gerasene Demoniac
(See Mark 5:1–20)

Jesus Brings Two Women from Death to Life

9:40 (See Mark 9:18–26.) In the stories of the two women healed, Luke omits Mark's observation that the woman had spent all she had on physicians and only grew worse. Ancient gospel commentators suggested that Luke as a doctor was partial to physicians—perhaps they had malpractice suits in those days also!

The Mission of the Twelve, 9:1 (See Mark 6:7–13)

Herod's Perplexity, 9:7 (See Mark 6:14–16)

Jesus Feeds Five Thousand People

9:10 (See Mark 6:30–44.) Mark and Matthew have two multiplications, one for Jewish Christians and another for Gentile Christians who become united by one bread. Instead, Luke has only one multiplication. However he will later have two apostolates, one by the twelve for Jewish Christians and one by the seventy disciples for the Gentile world. Both apostolates are united by the one word they preach.

Luke focuses more attention on the twelve (9:1, 10, 12). They take the initiative, organize the crowds and distribute the bread. This special emphasis on the twelve will continue at the last supper and in the Acts of the Apostles. There the special bond that unites the community is the breaking of the bread and the teaching of the apostles (1:42). Also, Peter's confession immediately follows the bread narrative as if connected with the teaching on bread. Because the meaning of Jesus' bread is so vital for this gospel, the narrative is linked to the final dramatic scene where Jesus is recognized by two disciples in the breaking of the bread. This link is made through the same introduction to the two stories: *The day was drawing to a close* (9:12; 24:29).

Peter's Confession of Faith

9:18 (See Mark 8:27–30; Matthew 16:13–20.) Again Luke records Jesus' prayer before momentous occasions. It is the master's prayer that makes Peter's confession possible.

Jesus Foretells His Death and Resurrection; Teachings on Discipleship

9:21 (See Mark 8:31–9:1.) With Luke's concern for the present moment, he records Jesus' saying about taking up the cross and adds **daily** for added emphasis. With the same focus on the present, Luke distinguishes between a future return of the Son of Man (26) and those **who will not taste death** before Jesus' return. This "seeing of the kingdom of God" already starts in Jesus' ministry and reaches a culminating point on the cross when he tells "the good thief" that **today** he will join him in paradise (23:43).

The Transfiguration of Jesus

9:28 (See Mark 9:2–9.) **While he was praying, the appearance of his face changed.** In this gospel, it is Jesus' prayer that causes this transformation and partially fulfills the promise about some who will see the kingdom of God come. Moses is strongly linked to this, for his face was illumined every time that he spoke to God on top of Mount Sinai (Exodus 34:29–35). **They saw his glory.** For the gospel audience, the effect of prayer will be a deep conformity with and imitation of Jesus' transformation.

The Healing of the Possessed Boy

9:37 (See Mark 9:14–27.) Luke centers his attention on Jesus as healer and his closeness to God, which has just been manifested on the mountain. Little is said about faith nor is there an explanation about why the disciples could not cure. The conclusion hints at Jesus' identification with God: **All were astonished at the greatness of God.**

Jesus Predicts His Death a Second Time

9:43 (See Mark 9:30–32.) Distinctive to Luke is the ending: **They did not understand this saying; its meaning was concealed from them.** Luke views the cross and its meaning as

God's secret to which no human being could attain, since it reverses all human values. Only the risen Jesus can explain it (24:25–26, 45).

The Christian Model and Image of the Child

9:46 (See Mark 9:33–37.) The image of the little child does not stand alone, but serves as a model for the whole journey narrative of 9:51 to 19:44. Luke is pre-eminently the gospel of children and "little ones" before God.

Jesus and Other Jewish Healers

9:49 (See Mark 9:38–41.) Here the above theme of "little ones" applies to an "outsider," a Jewish exorcist. Working miracles in Jesus' name is frequent in the Acts of the Apostles. But read the humorous example on the consequences of "faking it" in Acts 19:11–17.

PATHWAYS TO FURTHER DISCOVERY:

Only Luke mentions the women accompanying Jesus on his journeys (8:2–3). Why is Luke often called "the gospel of women"?

What leadership roles do women have in this gospel?

PERSONAL JOURNAL SUGGESTION:

Luke 9:18 describes Jesus' prayer. Study when and how Jesus prays in Luke's gospel. What effect could this have on your own prayer life?

THE JOURNEY NARRATIVE IN LUKE **9:51–19:41**

A Samaritan Village Refuses Hospitality

9:51 **When the days drew near for him to be taken up, he set his face to go to Jerusalem.** These words begin the long journey section in Luke. They contain instructions on how the audience can follow on the same way. This section contains the largest number of stories that are only in Luke. Here, the refusal of hospitality to strangers, especially prophets, was the most serious offense in ancient times. James and John (whom Jesus called "sons of thunder" in Mark) wanted to imitate Elijah the prophet who called down lightning on such people (2 Kings 1:9–16). Jesus had to turn and rebuke them. The Samaritan outsiders are an example of the theme of the "little ones" that introduces the journey narrative.

Difficult Decisions on Discipleship

9:57 (See Matthew 9:18–22.) Luke is much stronger on the cost of discipleship. It has priority even over the desire to care for aging parents and avoids delays that might be caused by farewell parties.

The Mission of the Seventy Disciples

10:1 Only Luke has this unusual mission. The number "seventy" symbolizes the whole world which the bible calls the "seventy nations." This originates in the image of seventy as a complete number. The command **Eat what is set before you** envisages a non-Jewish apostolate, since apostles of Jewish origin would hesitate to eat food that was not "kosher." Matthew's gospel (10:5) prohibited an apostolate to Samaritans and Gentiles. However, Luke is making a parallel to the two distinct missions in the early church. The first was that of Peter and the twelve who confined themselves mainly to reaching fellow Jews. The second was that of Paul and the seven "Greek assistants" to the twelve who went out to the Samaritans and ultimately to the Gentiles (Acts 6:1–8). Luke wants to show that Jesus is behind both apostolates.

The Return of the Seventy and the Rejoicing of Jesus

10:17 **The seventy returned with joy.** The feeling of joy pervades the whole gospel. However, Jesus says that there is joy deeper than that from charismatic powers. This joy is their membership in the messianic community: **Rejoice that your names are written in heaven**.

The rejoicing motif continues in Jesus' prayer of thanksgiving (see Matthew 11:25–27). Jesus has a deep inner joy because of his union with the Father. The chidren's theme continues as God turns away from the "wise and intelligent" and reveals his secrets **to infants**.

The Parable of the Good Samaritan

10:25 The lawyer's question introduces a new teaching that is put in parable form. The newness lies in putting together love of God and love of neighbor in one simple commandment. The unusual conclusion is that real love for someone in need is the same as love of God. The parable of the good Samaritan is only in Luke.

This parable has given rise to a host of good Samaritan hospitals and institutions, and this may confuse a modern audience. For Luke's audience, the Samaritan was not "good" at all, nor were the priests and levites "bad." The parable is really a comic paradox where the good become bad and the bad become good. The story describes a man who went down the treacherous road from Jerusalem to Jericho and was mugged by robbers. They stripped him of everything he had, beat him up and left him lying apparently dead at the side of the road.

If we put aside modern stereotypes, the people who came along were a good, holy priest and levite on the way to Jericho, a priestly city. These fine men were anxious to keep the law in every detail of their lives. The priest noticed the man by the wayside, apparently dead. If he were surely dead, the priest could not touch him because this would make him legally "unclean" and disqualify him from leading worship. This was a serious matter. In addition, purification could be a costly process involving a ceremonial bath in special holy water sprinkled with the ashes of a red heifer. It could be a financial disaster for the family. With their minds churning over legal requirements, the priest and the levite did not want to take any chances: each **passed by on the other side**.

Then the "enemy" and "bad person" came along, for that is

how Samaritans were considered (see Matthew 10:5). Not troubled by a mind whirling with religious regulations, he simply lets himself be moved by human compassion and acts accordingly. He works from his heart instead of his head. He even acts in a "foolish" manner: he puts aside everything else to care for the helpless victim. Pressed to leave for home, he even leaves a large sum of money with the innkeeper for his care, promising more if necessary on his return.

Jesus then explains that the real "neighbor" is **the one who showed him mercy.** To transfer this to a modern situation, we would have to imagine a holy minister, priest or nun as obviously good people preoccupied with "religion." This would be in contrast to someone like a drug dealer or pimp with no religion at all on his mind. The comic reversal and paradox then becomes clear: the good become the bad and the bad become the good.

Martha and Mary: Women's Roles as Disciples

10:38 This belongs to the many women's stories found only in Luke. It may be a counterbalance to the preceding good Samaritan parable. **He entered a certain village, where a woman named Martha welcomed him into her home.** This is quite unusual: Martha and Mary have their own home, and husbands or family are not mentioned. In the Acts of the Apostles, Luke tells of a woman named Lydia who headed a household (Acts 16:14–16).

As the older woman, Martha welcomes Jesus into her home and supervises the hospitality. Just seeing at least a dozen hungry disciples at the door quickly moved her to the efficient action for which years of experience had prepared her. Yet the younger sister Mary seems oblivious to all this. She just seats herself at the feet of the Lord, the attitude of a disciple (as in 8:35). The triple use of the word "Lord" strengthens the image of teacher and disciple.

Martha is busy and anxious about the needs of hospitality. She does not merely call Mary to help but appeals to Jesus for a command: **Tell her then to help me.** Luke has designed this story to answer questions in his church about women's roles.

The Lord's answer (and command) in this story speaks to this: **There is need of only one thing. Mary has chosen the better part, which will not be taken away from her.** We note that Martha is not condemned for her devoted role of hospitality, which is needed and much appreciated. However, the freedom of the younger sister to listen to Jesus and follow him has distinct priority over her duty to obey her older sister and assist in a traditional woman's role. Luke feels this is supremely important for the audience. In Luke, the new age will not come until women reach full equality in the work of the Spirit.

Jesus Teaches the Lord's Prayer

11:1 (See Matthew 5:9–13.) While this is in Matthew's sermon on the mount, Luke's setting has the disciples watching Jesus pray and wanting to imitate him. Luke writes, "Give us **each day** our daily bread." He is concerned to underline the very practical need of bread to eat for each day. The same Greek word for "each day" is here and in Acts 6:1 where it describes the meal "each day" provided for widows and the poor in the early church.

The Fruits of Persevering Prayer

11:5 Prayer pervades Luke's gospel and perseverance is an important part of it. This is illustrated humorously in a story about a man coming at midnight to request three loaves of bread. The request for three loaves even at midnight to feed an unexpected guest reflects the urgent priority of hospitality in the ancient world. Of course the friend protests at this most difficult request. Bread was always freshly made each day. To provide the bread, the whole household would have to be awakened. Fires in the oven would have to be rekindled. Women would have to begin the long laborious task to grind wheat, make it into dough, wait for it to rise and finally bake it. Hours would be needed. The request is absurd, but the importunate friend will not take "no" for an answer. No one in the house can sleep with the continual pounding and shouting at the door. So finally the friend gives in, even if only to obtain peace and quiet. The moral of the story attached to the Lord's prayer is significant: It is hard to refuse a determined, persevering request. If this is so with human beings, is it not preeminently so about God the **Father**, the friend of friends?

Matthew also has the saying about God being greater than any parent in giving gifts to his children (13). However, Luke changes one word for special significance. Matthew simply has prayer for "good things." Luke changes it to prayer for **the Holy Spirit**. Prayer for the gift of the Holy Spirit is prominent elsewhere as a model for the audience. Jesus prays for the Holy Spirit at his baptism (3:21) and the church prays for the Holy Spirit before the first Pentecost (Acts 1:19).

Jesus and the Prince of Devils, 11:14
(See Mark 3:22–27)

The Return of the Unclean Spirit, 11:24
(See Matthew 12:43–45)

Jesus Praises His Mother and True Disciples

11:27 This praise of Jesus' mother is only in Luke. Yet Jesus replies that the inner quality of her discipleship is even greater.

The Sign of Jonah, the Comic Prophet, 11:29
(See Matthew 12:38ff)

The Light of the Body, True Intentions, 11:33
(See Mark 4:21)

Jesus' Denunciation of Pharisees, 11:37
(See Matthew 23:1–36)

Exhortation to Fearless Confession, 12:1
(See Matthew 10:26–33)

The Parable of the Rich Fool

12:13 Jesus' reply to a request for settling an inheritance sums up the parable that follows: **Take care! Be on your guard against all kinds of greed; for one's life does not consist in the abundance of possessions.** Here is the story of a man who decided to build up a large "retirement fund" so in the future he could really sit back and enjoy life to the fullest. He presumed that his previous blessings in the form of material goods would surely lead to God's further blessing of a happy old age.

This is a striking "reversal" parable. Sudden death leaves the man with nothing, since everything is taken from him by others. Jesus concludes, **So it is with those who store up treasures for themselves but are not rich toward God.** The single-minded preoccupation with amassing possessions not only for present but for future use eliminates the total dedication to God that is requisite for the kingdom. The rich man is thus the poorest of all. If he had shared with others in view of the kingdom, he would have been truly rich. Instead, sharing is forced upon him by sudden death.

Cures for Worry and Anxiety

12:22 (See Matthew 6:25–33.) The previous parable about the dangers of wealth sets the stage for a counter-balance in trust of God to provide for those who labor for his kingdom. The conclusion is proper to Luke: **Do not be afraid, little flock, for it is your Father's good pleasure to give you the kingdom** (32). The greatest gift is that of the kingdom, and it is given to the "little ones," the models of the journey narrative. Other things do not matter that much, so Jesus says, **Sell your possessions and give alms.** Luke shows in his Acts of the Apostles how the early community put this in practice by selling property and possessions so that no one might go hungry (2:44–45; 4:32–37).

Responsibilities, Especially of Leaders

12:35 (See Mark 13:35; Matthew 24:43–44.) Like Matthew, Luke brings in the matter of a delayed return of the master

(Jesus). He also has much less severity than Matthew, where the master completely throws out the unwatchful servants. Instead, Luke has severe and light beatings depending on the amount of responsibility (47–48). Peter is specified by name (41). This suggests that Luke is especially concerned about the responsibilities of church leaders.

Jesus Asks for Difficult Decisions

12:49 (See Matthew 10:34–36.) **I have come to cast fire on the earth.** This is the refining, proving and separating power of fire through the word of the prophets and Jesus.

Times for Decision

12:5 Luke puts together sayings of Jesus from many sources to emphasize the importance of making good decisions before it is too late.

PATHWAYS TO FURTHER DISCOVERY:

How does the good Samaritan parable illustrate the approach of Jesus and of Christians in regard to the needs of people in the world?

PERSONAL JOURNAL SUGGESTION:

Note briefly the worries and anxieties that you face each day. Then apply Jesus' prescriptions for worry (12:22–34) to them.

Tragedies as Opportunities for Change

13:1 Luke reminds his audience that repentance is not a once and for all decision in the past. It must be renewed especially in times of unexpected tragedy. Jesus disagrees with the stereotype that these tragedies may be due to past sins. Tragedies are not payoffs for the past but present opportunities for change.

The Fig Tree and Repentance

13:6 Luke has no story of the cursing of the fig tree as in Mark and Matthew. Instead, he presents an image of patience and forgiveness with a renewed opportunity for change.

Jesus Heals a Crippled Woman

13:10 Women's stories are a specialty with Luke. He tells this story in beautiful detail. Actually, his Greek is the best in the New Testament. Here again he presents a striking contrast. Every farmer has special care for the animals, which were almost part of a household. This concern had priority over all sabbath laws. The story hints that women often did not receive such priority in farming households. There is also added symbolism in the story: Jesus makes the woman stand up free and tall instead of being bent over in humiliation.

Parables on the Yeast and Mustard Seed, 11:18–21
(See Mark 4:30–32 and Matthew 13:31–32)

Finding the Narrow Door

13:22 (See Matthew 7:31–32.) Luke softens Matthew's statement that only few can enter and writes instead, **Many will try to enter and will not be able**. Then warnings follow on the danger of complacency. The prophetic voice is always a challenge; it is never enough to claim familiarity with Jesus, past or present, with words like, **We ate and drank with you and you taught in our streets**. It is only faithful people in the past like Abraham, Isaac and Jacob and all the prophets who are saved, not a wholesale transaction. Others will come **from the east and the west** to take the places of those who rest on their laurels and fail to change. Those who think they are the privileged first will find themselves the last: **Some are last who will be first and some are first who will be last**.

Jesus Laments over Jerusalem

13:31 The Pharisees warn Jesus to leave Galilee where King Herod plans to arrest him, like John the Baptist. Jesus will leave but only to head for Jerusalem, the religious and civil capital. There, like many prophets before him, Jesus must be ready to suffer and even die. Yet Jesus loves Jerusalem and desires to gather them together **like a hen gathers her brood under her wings**. However, no religion offers an automatic guarantee of God's presence in its temple. Failure to hear the prophetic voice means desolation—an empty shell without a heart—until people listen once more and give the welcome greeting, **Blessed is the one who comes in the name of the Lord**.

Jesus Heals on the Sabbath and Tells Banquet Parables

14:1 Jesus was open for dinner invitations everywhere, whether with tax collectors or religion teachers such as here. Luke loves banquets: Jesus seems to be always at a free meal in his gospel and meals are often the setting for these teachings. Here three Lukan banquets follow. The first comes through a humorous observation on the way people compete to get the best seats near the host or important people. Jesus however sees the comical contrast to God's banquet where it is a unique privilege to be invited—a word repeated eight times in vv. 7–14.

This invitation is the supreme privilege of a lifetime. Those who realize this are simply overwhelmed with joy, knowing they could not possibly earn this in any way. Those who forget this and push themselves ahead of others land in the lowest place. This pride causes their downfall. On the contrary, those who renounce power-seeking find themselves unexpectedly pushed up by God. The story ends with Jesus' comic punch line: **All who exalt themselves will be humbled and those who humble themselves will be exalted**.

The above cue word "invite" leads to another parable. A true invitation to a feast is pure gift with no strings attached. Jesus describes a "feast of fools" by human standards. The guests are great hordes of the excluded "little ones," especially the poor and the disabled. These latter, especially **the crippled,**

the lame and the blind, were excluded from the temple because of their lack of physical integrity (often assumed to be caused by lack of moral integrity). In contrast, an invitation to special friends, relatives and rich neighbors is often like an investment with guaranteed returns. It pays off well in life, so why is God needed at all? Today, Luke would say that a church has only found Jesus when the handicapped and poor have the first place in people's hearts.

The Parable of the Great Supper

15:15 The third banquet parable has a counterpart in Matthew 22:1–10 and is from the common source "Q." Luke broadens the parable for wider application: **Someone gave a great dinner and invited many**. Such an invitation was a great privilege but required a considerable investment of time and preparation. In the story, many wise and calculating people made their excuses. One man said, **I have just been married; therefore I cannot come**. This was a serious excuse because newlyweds were exempt from military duty (Deuteronomy 20:7).

Of course the master was disappointed and angry, but there is no violent reprisal as in Matthew. The master's anger is only momentary and prompts him to be even more generous and far-reaching in his invitation: **Go out at once into the streets and lanes of the town and bring in the crippled, the blind and the lame**. (Once again Luke's concern for the disabled.) Unlike the wise, calculating people who make excuses, this group is overwhelmed with joy at such an unexpected and gracious invitation. They are already the excluded ones in society, so they ignore the risks and trouble involved.

However, the bounty of the host is never exhausted. The extent of his generosity seems as foolish as that of a person who would simply invite everyone in the phone book to a party. This is really a missionary command to go out to the whole world— to the excluded Gentiles. **Compel people to enter** is not an expression of force but one of oriental hospitality that will not take "no" for an answer. **That my house may be filled** sums up the master's (God's) purpose: The great final banquet hall of

God is not meant for a privileged few in a hall of many empty seats. It is literally meant to be a "full house" with every seat filled with the usually excluded poor and handicapped as well as vast "unclean" multitudes.

The Cost of Discipleship

14:25 Luke writes that it is not enough to follow Jesus as simply part of a **large crowd**. Difficult individual decisions must be made that involve "hating" others in the oriental sense of choice or preference. Luke has more on this cost of discipleship than any other gospel and illustrates it with similes of building a tower and organizing a military campaign.

Parables of the Lost Sheep, the Lost Coin and the Prodigal Son

15:1 Jesus' compassionate approach attracted many people with serious problems. This was shocking to many religion teachers who thoroughly screened anyone who wished to be a student. So they complained openly about Jesus' approach: **This fellow welcomes sinners and eats with them**. This statement introduces three more parables about how the audience should deal with "troublemakers." Each of these follows the same fourfold recognizable pattern: 1) a tragic loss in the form of a lost sheep, a lost coin or a lost son; 2) an anxious search in the form of a shepherd for a lost sheep, a woman lighting a lamp and sweeping the whole house, or the father looking along the road every day for signs of his wayward son; 3) a joyful finding where the word "found" is repeated; 4) a community rejoicing with either all the shepherds, the woman's friends, or a great party with orchestra, dancing and singing.

15:11 The third parable, the prodigal son, illustrates the above fourfold pattern. The title "prodigal" is misleading, for it means "extravagant" or "wasteful" and could hint at a very generous youth to whom our heart would go out. However, a careful reading reveals a young man who was a real thorn in his father's side. He asked for his family inheritance before it was due to him at his father's death, and the father was foolish enough to give it to him. The father's worst expectations were realized. He not only **squandered his property** that was part of their "social security" for old age, but he disgraced their name and reputation by **dissolute living**. Finally, he lost the last vestige of self-respect by taking a pig-feeding job from a Gentile farmer. This Gentile association implied a betrayal of his heritage and religion. He had really sunk to the lowest rung of disgrace.

At this point the reckless youth thought of his parents and his home—just when he had wasted all his inheritance and could be of no help to them. He resolved to return home and tell his father he was unworthy to be even called or treated like a son. **While he was far off, his father saw him and was filled with compassion; he ran and put his arms around him and kissed him.** In some ways, the father looks more like a "fool" than his son. It is difficult to even imagine him waiting each day for such a rascal to return.

Even a reluctant forgiveness would be more than the youth expected; he had no idea to what extremes his father would go. The old man ordered the best clothes for the boy and put a special ring on his finger. He then made plans for an extravagant party as if matching his son's wastefulness and extravagance. He hired an orchestra, singers and dancers. He ordered a sumptuous banquet to be prepared, using the fatted calf reserved for unusual, special occasions. Then **they began to celebrate**.

Now begins the contrast: the faithful older son had been working in the fields and was returning home after a hard day's work. When he drew near the house **he heard music and dancing**. On learning the reason, he was so angry that he refused to go in. His father understood how he felt and **came out to plead with him**. We can understand the older son's disappointment. He had worked hard as an obedient son for all these years, yet had never received such attention. His next words however betray something deeper: **When this son of yours came back who devoured your property, you killed the fatted calf for him.**

It is noteworthy that the elder son did not say "my brother" but "this son of yours" as if an outsider. The father appreciates what the older son has done over the years and acknowledges it. However, he replied that they had to celebrate because (in strong contrast) this *brother of yours* **was dead and has come to life; he**

was lost and has been found. The gospel audience can identify with this parable as an embodiment of what a "sacrament of reconciliation" means in practice. Parents can reflect with hope that the greatest gift they can give a child is the image of one who truly loves, just as God does. This will give strength and hope to a child in the darkest moments of his or her life.

PATHWAYS TO FURTHER DISCOVERY:

Using 15:1–32 as a model, plan a liturgy that could be dramatized for use in a community reconciliation ceremony.

PERSONAL JOURNAL SUGGESTION:

Compare carefully the three parables in 15:1–32 and list the parallel passages. Apply it to situations that you have experienced in your own life.

The Parable of the Dishonest Manager

16:1 Teachers and preachers have often avoided this story because it seems to praise the dishonesty of the property manager. Once again, a sense of humor furnishes a key for interpretation. The bible itself tells "humorous" stories about "shrewd operators." Jacob, the ancestor of the twelve tribes of Israel, was a cunning trickster, even disguising himself as his brother Esau in order to receive his father's last blessing. We may be amused in reading about the "how" of Jacob's trickery, but that does not mean we approve of everything that he did.

Here, the dishonest manager realizes he has been discovered and will receive a disastrous reckoning. What to do? His ingenuity in facing a real crisis makes us smile, although we do not approve his dishonesty. The steward makes "friends" for the future by slashing down all their bills and giving them big reductions. When the owner discovered what was happening, he smiled to himself and **commended the unjust dishonest manager because he had acted shrewdly** (8). Luke is telling his audience that in time of crisis they should really face it with every resource they have. He notes that people of the world often give far more attention to financial crises than believers do concerning God's kingdom.

Luke then applies the parable to the problem of money. He shows that we often have a hidden master in the form of money or material success. A drastic change is needed if God can truly be our master: **No slave can serve two masters** (13). The gospel points out that inner desires for money must be overcome, especially in religious leaders, because **God knows your hearts** (15).

The Rich Man and Lazarus

16:15 This Lukan story illustrates the previous discussion about money and riches, a topic Luke discusses more often than all the other gospels combined. The story is one of contrasts. The rich man regarded his riches as a sign of God's blessings, especially as he feasted sumptuously every day. In the same mentality, most people thought that Lazarus was suffering because of his sins, especially laziness. His sores and afflictions were an added sign, perhaps of secret sins.

The poor man died and was carried by the angels to be with Abraham. The dramatic contrast is immediately evident: the former beggar is now feasting and the rich man has become a beggar. The descriptions of afterlife may distract the modern reader to think that we have here only a traditional "pie in the sky" outlook. However, Luke is not primarily concerned with the furniture of heaven or the temperature of hell. He has already emphasized in the beatitudes the all-important **now** repeated four times in 6:20–25. So the dramatic reversal in the story concerns Jesus' new announcement of the kingdom. The poor instead of the rich become those blessed by God and they laugh with joy; the rich find themselves empty without a drop of water. **"God has filled the hungry with good things, and sent the rich away empty"** (1:53).

The Little Ones and the Humble in the Kingdom

17:1 (See Matthew 18:6–7.) This group centers about the "little ones" of Luke's great journey section. First of all, it emphasizes the seriousness of abusing them or leading them astray; next it moves on to "fragile ones" who fail frequently.

Similar to Matthew, Luke stresses the need of continuous, daily forgiveness. But in addition this gospel focuses on genuine efforts to change. Jesus repeats three times the necessity of **repenting**.

Finally, only Luke has the illustratory story about humble servants or little ones. Luke repeats this theme at intervals through his gospel. For example, Mary states that she is a humble servant of God (1:32) and that God looks favorably upon the lowly (1:53). Luke presents this attitude as that of Jesus— serving without hope of reward (6:35), not looking for medals and trophies.

Jesus Cleanses Ten Lepers

17:11 The ostracized lepers could only call out from a distance: "Jesus, Master, have mercy." Jesus directed them to go to the temple priests for certification of a cure and for the reconsecration necessary to take part in worship and community life. On the way they were cured. Nine of them gave priority to what they had to do to fulfill the laws governing their community re-entry. But one "foreigner" and Samaritan "wasted time" by first going to Jesus in joyful thanksgiving. This is a parable on priorities and the habit of blessing (thanksgiving). Jesus tells him, **Your faith has made you whole.** There is no further need for rituals (from which the Samaritan might be excluded as a "foreigner". Faith alone is enough.

The Coming of the Kingdom of God

17:20 **The kingdom of God is among you.** In contrast to exterior signs of God's kingdom, Jesus points to interior ones already at work. Luke also has this view in his second volume where the risen Jesus warns his disciples not to expect an external kingdom but the inner rule of the Holy Spirit (Acts 1:6). Yet the present does not stand alone but gives birth to the future. Jesus says, **You will long to see one of the days of the Son of Man** (22). The expression "day(s) of the Son of Man" derives from the biblical "day of the Lord," which is a future day of God's judgment or intervention.

17:22 Luke is also concerned that some Christians might overemphasize the present by saying that the awaited day is here with words like **Look here** or **Look there**. Consequently, Jesus states that the day of his return will come as clearly as lightning in the sky but only after he suffers and is rejected. The remaining illustrations, also in the other gospels, are reminders to be ready for Jesus' coming.

The Parable of the Persistent Widow and the Unjust Judge

18:1 The theme of judgment and second coming leads to this humorous parable. The persistent entreaties of the widow even wear out an unjust judge who is only concerned that his health can no longer take it. How much more will God then swiftly intervene in justice for those who **cry to him night and day**. The keynote word **justice** is repeated four times in this parable.

The Pharisee and the Tax Collector

18:9 The same justice theme now applies to God's work in justifying people by his kind mercy. Luke illustrates this by a parable with dramatic paradoxes. The Pharisee represents the extreme in goodness. He was a person who combined dedicated prayer with perfect observance of the law even in minute details. On the other hand, the tax collector represented the extreme in evil—a person who betrayed his own people by working for Roman oppressors and often cheated his own race.

There is nothing wrong with the Pharisee's prayer at first glance. He is a good man, thankful that he is different from ordinary sinful people. He fasts twice each week to make his prayers more intensive; he gives tithes on **everything** (12), even though a tenth of the oil, grain and wine would have been enough to satisfy the usual interpretation of the law. In contrast to this confident stance, the tax collector stood afar off, not even raising his eyes to heaven. He just kept beating his breast and asking God for mercy. The surprise ending is that this man returned home peaceful and **justified**, not the other. This illustrates the way God's justice operates in reverse to people's trust in their own efforts: **For all who exalt themselves will be humbled, but all who humble themselves will be exalted.**

Jesus Blesses Little Children

18:15 (See Mark 10:13–16; Matthew 19:13–15.) Children return again toward the end of Luke's journey instruction to emphasize that they are the model in the beginning, end, and throughout the believer's journey.

The Rich Government Official

18:18 (See Mark 10:17–22.) Only Luke has him as a member of the ruling class. Typically in Luke, Jesus asks him to sell **everything.** Jesus **looked at him.** In this gospel, Jesus also directs this look of grace and invitation to effect Peter's conversion (22:6). In response to Peter's question (28), only Luke mentions the possibility of leaving a wife for the kingdom.

Jesus Foretells a Third Time His Death and Resurrection

18:31 (See Mark 10:32–34.) Again, the Lukan theme that the mystery of the cross is completely incomprehensible to human beings without divine enlightenment.

Jesus Heals a Blind Beggar

18:37 (See Mark 10:46–52.) This story introduces Jesus' final ascent into Jerusalem in Matthew and Mark. Luke has it as a prelude to the story of Zacchaeus, someone whose eyes were actually opened to see who Jesus was.

Zacchaeus the Tax Collector

19:1 This story is the climax of Luke's great journey narrative. Unlike the rich ruler who went away sad (18:18), this man realized what was lacking in his life and did something about it. **He was short in stature** but climbed up a tree to see Jesus. It is hard to imagine Jesus without a smile as he looked into the tree, saw Zacchaeus, told him to come down and invited himself to dinner at the tax collector's luxurious home. Unlike the sad response of the rich ruler, Zacchaeus **was happy to welcome him.** Of course, everyone around was completely shocked: **he has gone to be the guest of one who is a sinner.** Zacchaeus, however, took a definite stand to make up for his notorious past. He not only decided to give half his goods to the poor but committed himself to a fourfold restitution to those he had cheated in any way. Zacchaeus is an audience model of the dramatic reversal necessary to become part of a kingdom where the poor laugh with joy and the rich go away sad.

The Parable of the Ten Talents

19:11 (See Matthew 25:14–30.) While Matthew's parable is similar, Luke has adapted his version in view of the preceding story. Zacchaeus has just made the risky investment of fifty percent of his capital on the poor, but the return has been overwhelming: **salvation has come to this house** (9). In this parable, those who really risk are those who gain five or ten times what they received. Not to risk is to run the danger of losing all like the slave who hoarded his money by wrapping it up in a piece of cloth.

Jesus' Triumphal Entry into Jerusalem

19:28 (See Mark 11:1–11.) Luke focuses on an entry of peace in contrast to that of a military hero. The crowds extend the angels' song *peace on earth* at Jesus' birth by singing **peace in heaven.** Jesus' completion of his Jerusalem journey foreshadows his ascension and return to the Father.

Jesus Weeps over Jerusalem

19:41 The theme of *peace* continues as Jesus sees the holy city from a distance (not only space but time). Jesus is not a hard-nosed prophet, but one who deeply feels the suffering of his people: **If you had only realized on this day the things that make for peace**. Then he describes the consequences of following military self-styled messiahs in a later war against Rome (66–71 A.D.). This is the direct contrast of following a leader of peace and non-violence. Luke is pre-eminently a gospel of these two themes.

Jesus Cleanses the Temple

19:45 The image of the messiah of peace continues as Jesus enters the temple. The symbolic driving out of merchants receives little attention. Instead, Jesus seems to take over and fulfill the temple's purpose for prayer and *teaching* (21:37). In the gospel beginning, this was foreshadowed when the child Jesus was found in the temple talking with the teachers and asking them questions. In the last verse of the gospel, the disciples, after Jesus' ascension, return to the temple for long periods of prayer.

PATHWAYS TO FURTHER DISCOVERY:

Trace the theme of the child/little ones through the journey section, 9:51–18:16. How does this help to illustrate the approach of Jesus?

PERSONAL JOURNAL SUGGESTION:

From the teachings of the journey section, draw up images of the life-style you would like to live in today's world.

The Authority of Jesus, 20:1
(See Mark 12:27–33)

The Parable of the Wicked Tenants, 20:5
(See Mark 12:1–12)

The Question of Paying Taxes, 20:20
(See Mark 12:13–17)

The Question about the Resurrection

20:27 (See Mark 12:18–27.) Luke has more detail in his version of this story. The question of new life is his special interest. He adds, **To him all of them are alive** (38). This suggests that the source of the resurrection is God's own life.

The Question about David's Son, 20:41
(See Mark 12:35–37)

Jesus Denouncing the Scribes, 20:45
(See Mark 12:38–40)

The Widow's Offering, 21:1
(See Mark 12:41–44)

The Destruction of the Temple Foretold

21:5 Luke, unlike Matthew 24:3, does not mention the end of time or the end of the world. Instead, he focuses on the temple to clearly separate its destruction from the return of the Son of Man. Yet Luke, like Mark, points out that the signs before the temple's destruction are similar to those before the final coming and should be a warning. However, the destruction of Jerusalem and the temple is only for a limited time in God's plans: **Jerusalem will be trampled on by the Gentiles until the times of the Gentiles are fulfilled** (24). At the end of this time, the Son of Man will return (25–28). The discourse ends with the words, **Every day he was teaching in the temple**. Luke does not have the other gospels' statements about the destruction of the temple and its replacement. Instead, he has the milder view that Jesus brings the temple to completion by his teaching activity in it.

The Plot To Kill Jesus

22:1 **Then Satan entered into Judas.** Here is the return of Satan that Luke predicted at the end of Jesus' first temptations in the desert (4:13). Luke views Satan as the mastermind behind Judas, the ruling authorities and Pilate. Jesus is fighting a cosmic battle to regain the world lost by our first parents whom God had called to "rule over the world" (Genesis 1:26). In Luke's passion account, Jesus will ask the audience to be with him in this cosmic struggle as part of the "Christian combat."

The Passover and the Institution of the Last Supper

22:7 (See Mark 14:12–25.) In view of his cosmic struggle motif, Luke expands the last supper story to make it a time of crisis and decision for all believers. First, he draws out the Passover background to make clearer links with Jesus' death. Jesus says, **I have greatly desired to eat this Passover with you before I suffer** (15). In Greek, there is a play on words in the term for "suffer." This word, *paschein*, is similar in sound to the word *pascha*, meaning Passover. Luke also preserves the Passover custom of several ritual cups of wine.

A second Lukan emphasis is on the central role of the apostles. **Peter and John** prepare the Passover (8). Jesus took his place at the head of the gathering and **the apostles with him**. Jesus says he will give them a kingdom so they might eat and drink with him and **sit on thrones judging the twelve tribes of Israel**.

A third emphasis is on the remembrance theme as Jesus says, **Do this in remembrance of me**. This is also a Passover theme. This feast is called a feast of remembrance (Exodus 12:14). The word has a strong meaning in Hebrew. To remember is to experience now God's presence and power. Therefore to remember Jesus in the breaking of bread is to bring to the present moment the fullness of his powerful presence. Throughout the gospel, Luke gives special attention to "remembering." This will come to a climax at the tomb where the risen Jesus prompts the women to *remember* (24:6).

The Disciples' Dispute About Greatness

22:24 Only Luke has this story at the last supper as one more opportunity for crisis solving. He sees the liturgy as a time of decision. Jesus acts as a servant when he gives his body/self for others in the last supper. Similarly, participants must serve one another. **A dispute also arose among them as to which one of them was to be regarded as the greatest.** This especially refers to eucharistic leaders who are to set an example for the others. Here Luke stresses the need to be like the youngest or little ones as they serve the community and to avoid lording it over them. In the Acts of the Apostles, the twelve follow this instruction literally. They wait on tables with their own hands until the work becomes too much for them alone (6:1–2).

Jesus Predicts Peter's Denial

22:31 (See Mark 14:27–31.) Continuing the theme of Christian combat, Jesus predicts Satan's return to tempt Peter. Only Jesus' prayer (as elsewhere in Luke) will enable Peter to pull through despite failure and be a "rock" to strengthen, literally "harden," others.

Instructions for Time of Crisis

22:39 This mysterious Lukan passage has baffled inter-preters over the centuries. Jesus first recalls the apostles' first mission when he sent them without purse, traveling bag and even sandals. Yet despite this they lacked nothing. This implies that they had enough because Jesus' presence through his word was with them. However, now he counsels them to buy whatever they need, even a sword. This seems to mean that, without Jesus' word and power, they will be left to their own resources and must literally fend for themselves. These words prepare for the disciples' coming armed defense in the garden without Jesus' permission. Yet even in this, God's plan in the scriptures will be fulfilled for they will be mistaken for revolutionaries or violent people: **he was counted among the lawless** (Isaiah 53:12).

Jesus' Agony on the Mount of Olives

22:39 (See Mark 14:32–42.) Luke begins and ends this short account with the same words: **Pray that you may not come into**

the time of trial. This announces a combat/temptation motif. As an example for the audience, Jesus can face arrest only by the power of prayer. **His sweat became like great drops of blood.** This reminds the audience of the struggles of our first parents because of their failure to obey God. They are told that **by the sweat of their faces** they shall earn their bread (Genesis 3:19). As in the first temptation scene (see 4:1–12), Jesus' struggle is not only for himself but for the whole human race.

The Betrayal and Arrest of Jesus

22:47 Here we find the temptation or prospect of failure in Luke's story. In Matthew and Mark, it is the desertion of all the disciples (Matthew 26:36; Mark 14:32). However, this desertion is omitted in Luke. Instead, the failure consists of disobeying Jesus by beginning an armed struggle without his orders; this would make the master appear like a militant revolutionary. The disciples do ask if they should resist but fail to await an answer before their violent response. Jesus has to intervene with a command to stop. He even heals the ear of the injured servant.

In view of this, the peaceful and non-violent Jesus acts in marked contrast to his violent, disobedient disciples. Jesus says, **This is your hour and the power of darkness.** Both the disciples and the crowd have fallen into the ways of Judas who became a tool of Satan (22:3) by trusting in the ways of power.

Peter Denies Jesus Three Times

22:54 In Luke's version, the initiative of Jesus is more prominent as **the Lord turned and looked at Peter**. This prompted him to remember what Jesus said and to weep bitterly over his betrayal (61–62).

The Mocking and Beating of Jesus
(See Mark 14:65)

Jesus Before the Council

22:66 (See Mark 14:53–64; Matthew 26:57–66.) In Luke's version of Jesus' trial, there is no accusation of blasphemy or statement that Jesus deserves death as in the first two gospels. However, the assembly brings Jesus before Pilate in the next passage and makes accusations before Pilate that could result in a Roman death penalty.

PATHWAYS TO FURTHER DISCOVERY:

Trace the theme of peace and non-violence as it progresses through the gospel of Luke. How could it be practical in today's world?

PERSONAL JOURNAL SUGGESTION:

How can Luke's description of the last supper help you to more fruitfully participate in the liturgy today?

Jesus Before Pilate and Herod

23:1 (See Mark 15:1–21.) Luke has the strongest gospel presentation of Jesus' innocence. The charge against Jesus is very clearly that of a revolutionary political messiah: "We found this man perverting our nation, forbidding taxes to the emperor, and saying that he himself is the messiah, a king." Pilate finds no basis for this and sends him to King Herod of Galilee who was in Jerusalem for the Passover feast. Their unusual agreement confirms Jesus' innocence. Luke's great concern about Jesus' innocence has two main reasons behind it. First, he wants to protect Christians from the possible charge that they are followers of a military revolutionary leader and a threat to Rome; second, the innocence of Jesus is a special biblical theme that we will discuss shortly.

Luke also has much more detail on the attempt of Pilate to have Barabbas as a possible substitute for Jesus. Twice Luke writes that Barabbas was not only guilty of starting a riot but was also a murderer (19, 25). Only Luke has Pilate, in another attempt to save Jesus, offer to have him flogged and then released.

The Crucifixion of Jesus

23:26 (See Mark 15:21–32; Matthew 27:32–44.) Luke introduces new people and events to help the gospel audience be part of all that is happening. We are part of **a great number of people (that) followed him**. First, there are the **daughters of Jerusalem**, the compassionate weeping women. Jesus tells them to weep not for himself but for their children. These little ones will suffer the future results of not following a messiah of peace: military, violent "messiahs" will bring on the horrible sufferings of the war with Rome.

In the last temptation of Christ, Luke has a triple crescendo of taunts about a helpless messiah who cannot even save himself, let alone others. The third temptation is even worse, coming from someone on another cross by Jesus' side who cries out, **Save yourself and us**. Luke calls them "criminals" to show the audience that the most unlikely and most desperate people can be affected. All have hope. Jesus' last words to any human being are addressed to a criminal who regretted what he had done and called out to Jesus for help in these words: **Jesus, remember me when you come into your kingdom** (42). These words are the representative voice not only of this person but of any human being in the worst possible situation.

As the last words of anyone speaking to Jesus before his death, each word has special significance. The name of **Jesus** has special power throughout this gospel. In Luke's second volume, the apostles proclaim that anyone calling on this name will be saved (Acts 2:21; 3:16; 4:12). **Remember**, we have seen, is a key word in this gospel. To "remember," as at the last supper (22:21), is to experience completely the Lord's presence and power. In regard to the **kingdom**, the "criminal" thinks that this time of power and completion will take place in the future. However, Jesus replies that it will all happen **today**—at the moment of Jesus' death.

Truly I tell you, today you will be with me in paradise. The "truly I tell you" stands for an "Amen" statement of Jesus with special significance in his own language. The "today" shows that Luke considers the moment of Jesus' death as initiating the coming of God's kingdom. A companion on the cross turns instantly into a perpetual companion in paradise.

The word "paradise" is a Greek translation of the Hebrew "eden," meaning pleasure or enjoyment. Only Luke uses this word. He shows that in this last statement of Jesus we find the concluding victory of the cosmic battle with Satan. The failure of Adam and Eve, the parents of the human race, has been reversed. Paradise has been reopened for the world through Jesus' death and forgiveness.

The Death of Jesus

23:44 (See Mark 15:33–41; Matthew 27:45–56.) **Darkness came over the whole land.** Both Mark and Matthew mention this darkness and the blackness and abandonment of Jesus' death. Luke adds the symbolism of the diabolical powers of darkness (22:53). However, a valuable clue to further meaning is the addition of the words, **While the sun's light failed.** Luke is linking the death of Jesus with God's prophecy in Joel 3:1, beginning with the words, **In the last days.** The prophecy announces a great outpouring of **the Spirit** on the human race, followed by specific references to all classes of people. As in Luke, the darkening of the sun is described, followed by the words, **Then everyone who calls upon the name of the Lord shall be saved** (3:5). This is parallel to the death of Jesus where the dramatic darkness of the sun follows immediately after the "criminal" calls upon Jesus' name. The splitting of the temple veil strengthens the all-inclusive theme (see Mark 15:38).

Jesus' very last exclamation is interpreted differently by each evangelist. Luke has **Father, into your hands I commend my spirit.** This is a dramatic echo of the very first words that Jesus uttered in the gospel. When his parents found him in the temple after a three-day search, his mother said to him, "Look, **your father** and I have been searching for you with great anxiety." Jesus replied, "Did you not know that I must be in **my Father's** house?" (2:49). Luke notes that Jesus' words were not understood at that time, but now they are comprehended through the cross.

The universal focus continues with the Roman centurion's praise of God and his declaration, **Certainly this man was innocent.** We have seen this innocence theme leading up to this climactic statement. We can now bring in its additional scriptural meaning with the help of Luke's second volume. There, Philip the evangelist meets an Ethiopian official returning from worship in Jerusalem. The official was reading the prophet Isaiah who described a just, innocent servant of the Lord giving up his life like a lamb led to slaughter (Acts 8:32–33; Isaiah 53:7–8). The centurion's words give hope to all who innocently suffer for what they really believe in.

They (the crowds) all returned home beating their breasts. This is another invitation for listeners to be part of the eternal drama of the cross. They "beat their breasts" in humble repentance as did the tax collector in 18:3. **But all his acquaintances, including the women…stood at a distance** (49). Unlike the first two gospels, women are no longer the sole witnesses at the cross. In line with this, Luke has omitted the fact (in Matthew and Mark) that all of Jesus' male disciples fled. Women, however, will have a unique but different role in the coming final gospel events.

The Burial of Jesus, 23:50
(See Mark 15:42–47)

The Resurrection of Jesus

24:1 (See Mark 16:1–8; Matthew 28:1–8.) **Why do you look for the living among the dead?** This question sums up a central teaching of this gospel that the risen Jesus is the Lord of life and death. This was already emphasized in the miracle of the raising of the son of the widow of Naim (7:11–17). Peter in the Acts of the Apostles calls Jesus **the author of life whom God raised from the dead** (3:15). The theme of new life completes the restoration of the garden of Eden and the tree of life. The first woman's name was "Eve," meaning "life," because she was "the mother of all the living" (Genesis 3:20). The many women (10) at the empty tomb reinforce the "life" theme as they witness the change from a cemetery of death to a garden of life.

Remember how he told you. The remembrance of both the scriptures and Jesus' word is a key motif running through Luke.

Then they remembered his word. The women have a central role in all these events by being the first to remember and therefore the first to experience. The women's role here is a more interior one in Luke, but without it nothing could have happened. They do tell what they saw at the tomb to the other disciples, **but these words seem to them an idle tale.** These words seem surprising unless we realize that Luke wants to center the external witness on Peter and the eleven in the events that follow.

Jesus Appears to Two Disciples on the Way to Emmaus

24:13 There were many manifestations or appearances of the risen Jesus that are not recorded in the gospels. St. Paul describes several of these when writing to the Corinthians (1 Corinthians 15:3–8). The gospels selected some of these not as relics of the past or as "scientific proofs" of Jesus' resurrection. Actually, Jesus' risen body was beyond physical laws. Even disciples and friends did not at first recognize him without some kind of sign or special words. The evangelists told these stories for teaching purposes and adapted them to show to audiences of any time how the risen Jesus manifests himself to them.

The story of meeting a stranger who explains the scriptures often became a reality as Christian traveling apostles moved from place to place. One such example is in the Acts of the Apostles when Philip the evangelist meets an Ethiopian official returning in his chariot from Jerusalem. Philip explained the scriptures to him and then baptized him (8:26–40). In Luke's story, the stranger (Jesus in disguise) asks the disciples what they had been talking about. After they explain the recent Jerusalem tragedy of Jesus' death, the stranger says, **How slow of heart (you are) to believe all that the prophets have declared** (25). The stranger then explains all in the scriptures relating to Jesus and his death. Luke has been leading his whole gospel up to this point. God's secret of salvation through the cross is a plan that no human being could fathom—only the risen Jesus could reveal it.

Luke has carefully paralleled the beginning and end of the gospel according to dramatic techniques. Before the birth of

Jesus, his parents found no hospitality at the inn: **There was no place for them at the inn** (2:7). At the end of the gospel, in contrast, the mysterious stranger receives an offer of hospitality and reveals himself as the risen Jesus (29–31).

At the birth of Jesus, the sign of the manger showed that the child Jesus was the true source of bread and nourishment. At the gospel ending, Jesus reveals himself in the breaking of bread (31). This becomes the time when the early church continues to experience his presence (see Acts 2:42; 20:7). Thus Luke presents two ways that the risen Jesus is always found: through the explanation of the scriptures and through remembering him as they break bread.

Jesus Appears to All the Disciples

24:36 This is a final vision to Peter along with the others (34–35) centering about the all-important reality of Jesus' presence. Is the risen Jesus a phantom or a ghost (37, 39)? This is especially significant for a Greek audience that might have trouble with the bodily reality of Jesus after his resurrection. At the tomb, Luke was specific: they did not find the **body** (24:3). In this final vision, one sign of Jesus' real presence is the showing of his **hands and feet** with all the physical marks of crucifixion. Another is Jesus actually eating in their presence. Luke is the strongest New Testament writer on the very tangible reality of Jesus' risen body. Yet at the same time, Luke notes that close disciples did not recognize him until he made himself known. His risen body also had qualities not present in an ordinary person, for he disappeared right after the breaking of bread and then reappeared after the two disciples brought the news to Peter and the rest.

Then follow the final words and commission of Jesus to his disciples. Just as the secret meaning of the cross in the scriptures was opened for the disciples, now it is repeated for Peter and the others. This ends with the commission that **repentance and forgiveness of sins is to be proclaimed in his name to all nations beginning from Jerusalem**. Here again the message of universal forgiveness began with John the Baptist (3:3–6) and now the gospel ends with the same note. Jesus' very last words are really an introduction to Luke's second volume: **And see, I am sending upon you what my Father promised; so stay in the city until you have been clothed with power from on high.**

The Ascension of Jesus

24:50 In this final gospel scene, Jesus returns to his Father in heaven. Jesus raises his hand and blesses them with the gesture of a high priest. This blessing is especially for the gospel audience; it is to energize them with the words and power of the gospel they have just heard. The gospel opening and closing come together. It began with all the people outside the temple waiting in vain for Zechariah the priest to come out and give his blessing. Now at the end of the waiting period, Jesus goes into his heavenly temple and blesses them. The disciples return to the Jerusalem temple where they await their empowerment for a mission to the world. Some ancient manuscripts end with an "Amen," the natural positive "so be it" response of an attentive audience.

PATHWAYS TO FURTHER DISCOVERY:

What special meanings of Jesus' death does Luke give his audience in 23:26–49?

PERSONAL JOURNAL SUGGESTION:

Imagine the scenes and listen to the words of the risen Jesus in Luke 24. How do they tell you how to recognize his presence in your life?

PART IV
THE JESUS STORY:
THE VOICE OF JOHN

Introduction

John is so different from the first three gospels that these latter are called the *synoptic* gospels, from syn/optic, "seen together." This is because the first three gospels when put side by side in columns often resemble one another. John wrote after these first three to balance them and give special attention to the divine side of Jesus as the eternal Word of God. This Word of God came down to earth and became human. His mission was to bring others to a correspondingly high appreciation of their own "divinization" as children of God and then to return to God the Father with them.

In the other gospels, more weight on the balance is placed on the first or "external" journey of Jesus from his baptism or birth to his death in Jerusalem. In the fourth gospel, the balance is more on the second or "interior" journey of the divine Word ever present in Jesus. When Jesus returns to the Father, he leaves behind for others his own inner Spirit or Paraclete (chapters 14–16). This Spirit duplicates and continues all that Jesus did so that each disciple becomes a "twin" of Jesus. This journey of the Spirit working in each disciple might be called the "third journey" of Jesus. The gospel of John is set up in a journey format so that the audience may make this third journey together. The model for the journey of the audience is the "beloved disciple," or the "other disciple," as he sometimes designates himself. He is the source or author of this fourth gospel as well as the ideal disciple for an audience of any time.

Our author is concerned about the diversity of views that some Christians have about Jesus. For example, some considered him as little more than a messiah, a superlative human being and sign worker. Others thought him to be so divine that he was hardly a human being at all. Our writer wants to share his own very lofty views of Jesus with the gospel audience. He describes Jesus as divine with the most explicit statements of the New Testament. At the same time he will present Jesus as truly human and dying on the cross to be a sacrificial lamb of God bringing forgiveness and salvation to all. Such beliefs in Jesus would be hard to retain in a Roman world of the early second century. Roman decrees required everyone to worship the emperor as "Lord and God." Severe consequences, not excluding arrest and death, faced those who did not comply. From beginning to end, the audience will learn how to face such challenges.

SUGGESTIONS FOR STUDY:

Read over the entire gospel of John in one or two sittings. As you read, note how this gospel portrait of Jesus compares or contrasts with that of the first three gospels. Before studying the explanations of any gospel section, first read slowly the gospel text itself.

The Gospel According to John

The Gospel Prologue

1:1 Here we have an initial summary of the gospel's deeper understanding of who Jesus is and what he wants to accomplish. Instead of Jesus' exterior journey from birth to death, we have the eternal journey of the Word into human history.

In the beginning was the Word. The first sentence of the bible, describing God's creation, starts with similar words **In the beginning...God created the heavens and the earth**. To begin the work of creation, God spoke his word, **Let there be light**, in order to dispel the primordial darkness. In the biblical view, God's speech or word is the creative energy supporting the universe. As supporting all life, especially human beings, it is called *spirit* or breath. In the gospel Greek, "word" is *logos*. In the Greek world, this word had a meaning among many philosophers as referring to the inner reason (logos) that unified and directed all of creation. So the biblical meaning could resonate well with this Greek view.

The climactic moment of the journey of the *Word* through history was when the **Word became flesh and lived among us** (14). Thus people could see the glory (divine manifestation) of this *Word* in a human being the audience knows is Jesus. The expression "lived" is literally in Greek, "pitched his tent," which recalls how God through the Hebrew ark of the covenant originally stayed with his people in a movable tent to accompany them.

However, not everyone recognized the Word in creation or in Jesus, even among those closest to him. **But to all who**

received him...he gave power to become children of God.
Thus Jesus gave to all who received him the *gift* to be what he
was by *nature*, a child of God. This is a new second birth and
creation that does not come from a human source. It is not **of
blood** (ancients considered the blood of the womb as the place of
conception) nor the result of human desires, **but of God.**

Throughout biblical history there has been a progressive
preparation for this outcome: **The law indeed was given
through Moses** (17), but no one has really seen God to the fullest
extent. **It is the only Son who is close to the Father's bosom
who has made him known.** In the bible the word "bosom" was
used of intimate relationships such as child to parent or husband
and wife, e.g., "the child of my bosom." Here, Jesus as Son, with
his intimate relationship to his Father, is qualified to make
known to the audience who God really is.

Parallel to Jesus, the beloved disciple, described as "at the
bosom of Jesus" (13:23), can reveal Jesus to others, which he does
through this gospel. Over the centuries, this beloved disciple has
been identified with John, one of the twelve apostles. Today,
however, most scholars regard him as outside the circle of the
twelve and bringing out aspects of Jesus that are quite distinct
from what we find in the first three gospels. When we refer to
the author as "John" in this work, we are really considering the
beloved disciple, not one of the twelve, as the source of this
gospel.

The Testimony of John the Baptist

1:19 In the synoptic gospels, John the Baptist is a fiery
messenger of repentance who baptizes Jesus and introduces
him. Here the Baptist is only someone who introduces Jesus and
announces what Jesus' mission will be. Jesus' baptism is not
even directly mentioned. **This is the testimony given by John.** It
is an official one given to leaders sent from the Jerusalem capital.
John is the first important witness (Gk., *martyr*) well known to
the audience as an example of someone who gave his life for
what he believed in. The Baptist is so important and well known
that he must deny the authorities' questions about whether he is
the messiah, Elijah returned or the expected future prophet.

The Baptist's Testimony to Jesus as Lamb of God

1:29 Here is the Lamb of God who takes away the sin of the world. The Baptist repeats this in 1:35 and thus introduces a dominant gospel theme. The blood of the paschal lamb sprinkled upon the people's homes saved them from death in Egypt (Exodus 12:13). The gospel will conclude with Jesus offering himself on the cross as the new paschal lamb. Note that the Baptist says *sin* of the world, not *sins*. The *sin of the world* does not consist of single transgressions but is a fundamental lack of believing and openness to God. **The world** or **everyone** (1:6, 9) is a constant universal emphasis in John in opposition to any kind of religious exclusiveness.

John testified that Jesus was **before me** (30) though he seemed to come after him. This is because Jesus was the eternal Word. The Baptist also says that Jesus has the abiding Spirit of God as prophesied by the prophets (Isaiah 11:2). The Spirit remained on Jesus so he could bestow this Spirit on others. This Jesus will do in a final gospel scene when he will appear and say, **Receive the Holy Spirit** (20:22).

The First Disciples of Jesus

1:35 This "fourth gospel" informs us that Jesus' first apostles were previously disciples of the Baptist who introduced them to Jesus. The Baptist had a widespread influence, and we read about some of his disciples in Acts 18 and 19. Much attention is given to the disciples' call as a typical pattern at any time. They are the first examples of Jesus "living among us," noted by the gospel prologue (1:14). Various English translations of this central gospel theme are "abide," "stay," "remain," "dwell," etc. All of them translate one Greek verb used of God's dwelling with his people in a movable tent and then in the temple in Hebrew history. A disciple is one who abides with Jesus and forms a close relationship with him.

One of these two disciples is Andrew (40), brother of Peter. The other is mysteriously unnamed. He appears to be the "other disciple" or beloved disciple who is the source of this gospel. He is also the ideal disciple that the audience can identify with as they accompany Jesus on the journey that he is about to begin. This is the "third journey" we have already mentioned. Thus a reader can take part in all the events, meet all the people on the way and be part of a learning experience. John's gospel is eternal drama transcending space and time. This is a unique feature of this gospel.

For the Greek-speaking audience, the Hebrew "messiah" is translated into "Christos," meaning "Anointed One" (41). In Matthew's gospel we read in detail about the new name of Simon and its significance (16:13–20). Here John preserves the original Aramaic word "Cephas," a Hellenized form of *Kepha*, meaning "rock."

1:43 **The next day Jesus decided to go to Galilee.** Jesus decides to break away from the narrow confines of the Jordan River and John's baptizing ministry to engage in a much broader apostolate. He assembles his fellow travelers for the journey—a signal to the audience to be ready to accompany him. Then follows a list of the various titles of Jesus that will be revealed during the journey: messiah, prophet, Jesus of Nazareth, Son of God. However, some big surprises lie ahead. Jesus is far greater than any of these. His mysterious vision of Nathanael under a distant fig tree hints at this, but it is not enough. Jesus tells the audience that they will see the heavens opened and **the angels of God ascending and descending upon the Son of Man** (51).

The above key scriptural text is familiar to the audience from the story of Jacob's ladder (Genesis 28:10–17). Jacob/Israel had to flee from home and feared for his life after deceiving his brother Esau in obtaining his father's special blessing and inheritance. Jacob stopped to rest and pray at the ruins of Bethel, a holy place. That night he dreamed of a ladder going all the way up to heaven. Angels were carrying his prayers up to God and returning with God's gifts and answers. God revealed himself to Jacob and promised to be with him and protect him on his long journey to find a wife among his kinfolk and then return to his parents' home in Israel. God promised to prove his presence by special signs along the journey. The first was a wedding which made possible the beginnings of God's people in the twelve tribes of Israel. To make possible the wedding there was an unusual water miracle by which Jacob was able to recognize his future wife (Genesis 29:1–14).

Jesus' journey is modeled on that of Jacob from a literary standpoint. Jesus begins the journey recalling the start of Jacob's journey with the vision of Jacob's ladder. Just as God accompanied Jacob and helped him with great signs, so also God will manifest his presence in Jesus through seven major signs and many minor ones. The first, parallel to Jacob's wedding, will be the marriage at Cana of Galilee where there will be an even greater water miracle when Jesus changes water to wine.

THE BOOK OF INCOMPLETE SIGNS (2:1–12:50)

In the synoptic gospels, we learned about many healings, exorcisms and other miracles of Jesus. John (throughout, this will be the author, not one of the twelve) instead uses the word "sign." This means a word, gesture or action suggesting a special deeper meaning. In this gospel, Jesus' miracles are the setting for such signs. This sign moves from the present, e.g. cure, to what Jesus wants to do for the audience of any time as a result of his "hour." This will be the time of his death, resurrection and gift of the Holy Spirit.

Often, this sign meaning is conveyed through a double or deeper meaning in Jesus' words. The perennial audience can clue into this deeper level through trust and believing in him. In John, we find a sequence of seven principal signs beginning with the wedding of Cana, which is the first (2:11). Jesus can convey these double sign meanings because of the "double level" of his life. He is indeed the same human Jesus we saw in the other gospels. However, at the same time he is the eternal Word at work in the world right from the first verse of the gospel. A miracle becomes like a setting in which a person can go behind the external scene and enter into a deep relationship with Jesus as the Word of God.

The Wedding at Cana

2:1 **There was a wedding in Cana of Galilee.** Immediately we enter the world of the symbol. Every wedding, as a covenant, mirrored something of God, the author of covenants, especially marriage (Genesis 1:27–28; 2:24). The bible describes God's relationship to his people in terms of an espousal. For example, the prophet Hosea announced in God's name, **I will take you as my wife forever** (2:21). John the Baptist will describe Jesus as a bridegroom (3:29). Jesus' goal is to celebrate the final messianic wedding feast promised by the prophets.

The mother of Jesus was there. She will be an important link between two levels of meaning: she is present at the earthly event at Cana; she will also be present at the "hour" of Jesus on the cross that she will witness (19:25–27). Although Mary had been dead for many years by the time of the gospel writing, she is still very important for the gospel audience. This is because of her closeness to her son both as a mother and as a witness and participant at the cross.

When the wine gave out. Abundant free wine for everyone was the principal feature of the week-long wedding celebration. It would be a lifelong disgrace if a couple's marriage was remembered as the one where the wine ran out. At another level, this is a hint that God's messianic marriage will require a special new vintage.

The mother of Jesus said to him, "They have no wine." These are words of trust. However, here and throughout John, trust in Jesus as a miracle/sign worker is not enough. Consequently, Jesus hesitates to act only on this level and moves to a deeper meaning: **What concern is that to you and to me? My hour has not yet come**. The key words are **my hour**. Only Jesus' time or "hour" of triumph on the cross will make possible the **wine** that he really wants to give. Wine, with its stimulating effect, is symbolic of the Spirit. Even today, liquor is sometimes called "spirits" to convey this mysterious powerful ingredient.

Despite Jesus' hesitation, Mary continues to believe. She represents the church/community. **She said to the servants: Do whatever he tells you.** These are covenant words (Genesis 41:55). The miracle and new wine for the audience can only come through doing what Jesus says, impossible though it may seem. (Water to wine really stands for the impossible.)

Now standing there were six water jars. These huge water containers were for the customary Jewish ritual hand washings before meals. The imperfect number "six" may represent the change from the old age to the new that Jesus wants to accomplish. The enormous quantity of resulting wine signifies the superabundant gift of God. **Jesus said, "Fill the jars with water." ...And they filled them to the brim.** The main point is exact obedience to Jesus' word in doing so and then bringing the jars to the chief steward. **The chief steward...did not know where it came from.** The idea of a mysterious source is a gospel refrain to show there are divine sources not available to human beings (see 4:11).

You have kept the good wine until now. This "good wine" symbolizing the Spirit is God's long-awaited gift in the messianic age. This first sign teaches "the other disciple"/ believers that this wine is always available when they duplicate the gospel instructions: they must come together to celebrate God's wedding banquet, ask with the same trust as Mary, remember Jesus' *hour*, and do what he tells us to do. This meaning will be manifest on the cross when Jesus obeys his Father in taking the cup of wine (according to the scriptures) and when the blood and water from his side are recognized as a sign of his gift of the Spirit. Believers imitate Jesus' own obedience to his Father.

Jesus Cleanses the Temple

2:13 (See Mark 11:11–17; Matthew 21:12–13; Luke 19:45–46.) **The Passover of the Jews was near.** In addition to signs, the fourth gospel uses the Jewish feasts, especially Passover, to bring out the deeper meaning of Jesus' ministry. The great feature of Passover was the sacrifice of the Passover lamb and the Passover meal. In the other gospels, the temple cleansing takes place just before the end of Jesus' life. Here it occurs at the beginning with some special shades of meaning. **He drove all of them out, both the sheep and the cattle.** Only John has this complete "cleanout" of the sacrificial animals. In view of what follows, this symbolizes that Jesus will replace them since he will be the new temple and Passover sacrifice.

People naturally asked what sign from God would support his action in the temple. Jesus replied, **Destroy this temple and in three days I will raise it up**. This is a typical double meaning Johannine statement. It is misunderstood in terms of the present temple structure, so the author adds for the audience: **He was**

speaking of the temple of his body. Following this we can observe the process of the church's understanding of Jesus' words: **After he was raised from the dead his disciples remembered that he had said this.** This is a post-resurrection understanding of mysterious words of Jesus not understood in his earthly life. **Many believed in his name.** Jesus then explains that this is a belief based on miracles/signs that is imperfect. Consequently, Jesus cannot yet entrust himself in a total relationship.

The Night Visit of Nicodemus

3:1 Besides signs and wonders, the audience/anonymous disciple learn from every person met on the journey. This is somewhat like the great traveler Ulysses who says (in Tennyson's poem), "I am part of everyone I have met." The first person met after the Cana wedding is Nicodemus. Coming secretly **by night**, he represents secret believers in Jesus because of his miracles, for he says, **No one can do these signs that you do apart from the presence of God.** Nicodemus had thought he could simply add his belief in Jesus as a teacher and sign worker to his traditional Judaism.

Jesus replied that additions are not enough—it must be a completely new start: **No one can see the kingdom of God without being born from above** (or again). This statement is the origin of the phrase, "a born-again Christian," meaning a complete change of life-style rather than a mere cultural, automatic matter through a purely ritual baptism not connected with life.

No one can enter the kingdom of God without being born of water and Spirit (5). The textual note explains that the same Greek word *pneuma* is used for both spirit/breath and wind. This is because the ancients believed that the earth was truly alive and breathing with the breath/Spirit of God. Nicodemus finds all this hard to believe because he does not recognize that Jesus has come down as a heavenly Son of Man and revealer of God's secrets to people on earth (13).

In verse 14, Moses had healed the people during a plague by lifting a serpent on a cross for all to look at (Numbers 21:4–9).

So must the Son of Man be lifted up. This means that in God's plan, the disgraceful and humiliating "lifting up" on the cross will be changed into a literal "raising on high," or exaltation. This view is drawn from the prophet Daniel's Son of Man passage in 7:1–14. There the suffering Son of Man, representing Israel as humiliated by the Greeks, is raised to God's side in judgment and triumph.

That whoever believes in him may have eternal life. The verb "believe," never the noun "belief," occurs over a hundred times in John as the gospel focuses on a permanent personal relationship with Jesus. **Whoever** or equivalent expressions constantly recur, expressing the great universal thrust that is open to the whole world. **Eternal life,** found seventeen times in John, is not a "pie in the sky" concept. The first verses of the gospel state, **In him was life.** Relationship with Jesus as Word of God and source of life can never be broken, even by death (11:25). The great motivating force behind all this is: **God so loved the world that he gave his only Son** (16). The biblical image is that of Abraham giving his only son Isaac to God, even though it could mean death (Genesis 22).

What follows in verses 17–21 expresses the outlook on time in the fourth gospel. Relationship with the eternal Word is permanent and thus brings the future into the present. Consequently, many future statements of the synoptic gospels are no longer in John. The future judgment, for example, takes place now as people make their present decisions. Jesus as light (1:4) comes into the world to expose darkness and its deeds. Those with courage expose their deeds to that light and thus escape any fear of future judgment.

Jesus and John the Baptist

3:22 Here we find that both Jesus and the Baptist continued their apostolate of repentance and water baptism. The discussion shows that Jesus was eclipsing John in popularity. However, John is not sad but joyful as a **friend of the bridegroom** who stands by and rejoices. The stern image of the Baptist found in the synoptics is no longer present in the fourth gospel.

Jesus the One from Heaven

3:31 This passage is an example of Jesus' gradual identification with God as it takes place in this gospel. This leads to a seeming exclusivism: **Whoever believes in the Son has eternal life**. However this is not directed toward outsiders, but to some in the Christian audience. The author wants to raise them to the highest possible understanding of Jesus' person.

PATHWAYS TO FURTHER DISCOVERY:

1. For the wedding feast of Cana, 2:1–12, look carefully through this story of Jesus' first sign. What symbols and images do you find in this story? What higher meaning do they have in view of Jesus' hour?

2. In comparison to Mark 1:16–20, what special meaning does the call of a disciple (1:35–51) have in this gospel?

PERSONAL JOURNAL SUGGESTION:

In view of the story of Nicodemus (3:1–21), what does it mean for you to be a "born again" Christian?

Jesus and the Samaritan Woman

4:1 The most fascinating person we meet on the journey is the notorious woman of Samaria. (For the hostility between Jews and Samaritans, see the comments on Matthew 10:5.) Like the beloved disciple, the woman is anonymous so the audience can identify with her. The conversation is really an instruction that readers can apply to themselves.

Jesus was alone, tired, hot and thirsty, hoping that someone would come along with a bucket so he could get a drink from the well. He completely shocked the Samaritan woman by asking her to give him a drink. This was shocking first of all because she was a woman and it was unheard of for a man to address a lone woman in public (see 4:27). Secondly, she was considered ritually unclean, like a Gentile; Jesus would make himself unclean by drinking from the same jar or bucket. The story illustrates how the accompanying reader must break every social barrier in the way of associating with others.

How is it that you, a Jew, ask a drink of me, a woman of Samaria? Jesus, as usual, moves the conversation to a deeper level: **If you knew the gift of God...you would have asked him, and he would have given you living water.** "Living water" (from a spring, symbolizing "Spirit") is vastly superior to well water. Sharing this kind of water would lead to a deep relationship, which is what Jesus offers. But the woman does not yet understand on this level. How can Jesus do this? Jesus has no bucket and **the well is deep** (a hint of a deeper meaning or source). It all seems so impossible. Is he greater than their ancestor Jacob who gave them this well?

Jesus explains the nature of this new water that completely quenches thirst forever and gives eternal life. Finally the woman asks (and the audience on the journey with her) **Sir, give me this water.** We note the once and for all nature of this gift, signifying Spirit.

The humorous dialogue that follows illustrates the steps any disciple must take to achieve a deep relationship with Jesus. First there must be honesty and truth. The woman is willing to face the embarrassing details of her past life: five previous marriages and now a union outside wedlock. Jesus had said previously that deeds must be brought out of darkness into light in order to dispel darkness (3:20). She also asks about another obstacle: her ancestors as Samaritans had been excluded from worship in Jerusalem; consequently, they worshiped at a holy site on a mountain near Samaria. Jesus replies that no particular place can ever be an exclusive place of worship. He offers a new type of worship that is deeply interior and based on **spirit and truth** (23). Yet Jesus acknowledges his own roots and those of the audience: **salvation is from the Jews** (22). While there is conflict with institutional religious leaders of the Jews in this gospel, there is a deep appreciation of the divine origin of Judaism.

The woman then expresses the common belief of both Samaritans and Jews in a coming messiah (25). Jesus replies, **I am he.** It is a surprise for the audience that the first person in this gospel to whom Jesus reveals his identity is a woman. Her sharing of secrets is matched by Jesus' sharing of his own greatest secret. Thus, we have the roots of a deep relationship. The disciples' surprise at Jesus' speaking with a woman (27–28) is shared by those in the audience who need more appreciation of women's leadership. This woman becomes the first apostle in this gospel to go out and bring good news to others. She leaves behind her precious water jar (symbolizing her former life and limitations?) and with disarming, contagious honesty tells everyone: **Come and see a man who told me everything I have done. Can he be the messiah?** (29).

The hungry disciples do not catch the deep significance of all this and want Jesus to start eating (so they can begin to eat also?). But Jesus replies in a mysterious manner: **I have food to eat that you do not know about.** Jesus' inner source of nourishment is his mission from God to bring others food, drink and energy for eternal life. **Do you not say, "Four months more and then comes the harvest"** (35)? This was a common proverb expressing that people like to build dreams of happiness for the future, whether for graduation, a better job, retirement, etc. Jesus replies that the future is now—the fields are already ripe for the future. This is because Jesus is looking to the distance and seeing people coming to him because of the Samaritan woman's witness (and many other women like her).

Many Samaritans from that city believed in him (39). The first breakthrough of the gospel to a virtual non-Jewish world comes through a woman missionary. She makes possible the goal of Jesus in the gospel prologue (1:14) to **stay with them** (40). The conclusion, "We know that this is truly the **Savior of the world**," emphasizes the universal impact of the story. John's gospel is the strongest of the four about women's leadership, of which this is the first example.

The Second Sign: The Healing of the Royal Official's Son

4:46 This second gospel sign is the healing of a royal official's son. It is a further movement from Samaria out to the world. The story has similarities to the healing of the centurion's servant in Matthew 8:5–13. There Jesus likewise heals from a distance by the power of his **word**. This **word** has just been demonstrated in the previous story's conclusion (39–42). The power of this word even to restore life to the dead is emphasized by the fivefold repetition of the death to life theme. This sign resembles the sixth sign in chapter 11 that features the power of Jesus' word to raise the dead Lazarus.

The Third Sign: Jesus' Healing on the Sabbath

5:1 The third gospel sign is Jesus' healing on the sabbath. In this story, an unfortunate man had been paralyzed for thirty-eight years; he was awaiting a cure through the occasional therapeutic stirring of the waters in the Sheep-Gate pool. Jesus said to him, **Stand up, take up your mat and walk** (8). The main issue is that work such as carrying objects was strictly prohibited on the sabbath. Consequently, Jesus was severely criticized for such a cure.

However, Jesus' supreme rule is imitation of God, which is above all laws and regulations: **My Father is still working and I am working** (17). Although the bible stated that God "rested" on the sabbath (Genesis 2:2), everyone realized that God had to continue his loving care of the universe every day of the week. This was the sole model of Jesus despite all the sabbath day laws. Therefore "the Jews" (which usually represents the civil and religious authorities in John) **were seeking all the more to kill him because he was not only breaking the Sabbath...**(the infraction of some sabbath laws was punishable by death) **but was calling God his own Father, thereby making himself equal to God** (18). This reflects a time situation around sixty years after Jesus' death when Christians' worship of Jesus as God provoked blasphemy charges against them. The gospel of John makes explicit what was only hinted at by Jesus' extraordinary closeness to God during his earthly life. The accompanying audience on the Johannine journey learns that their supreme "law" is imitation of God and Jesus, even though this may risk a dangerous confrontation with authorities.

Jesus' Imitation of the Father

5:19 The ideal of imitation of God (which Jesus took from Judaism) continues in the following proverb: **The Son can do nothing on his own, but only what he sees the Father doing.**

This is a craftsman's parable, taken from the way careers and professions were learned in those days—from parents.

A mother taught both boys and girls until the age of twelve years. After that age, young women would learn household duties from their mothers and boys would learn the secrets of a trade from their fathers. The way to learn was through "in-service" training—"hands on" work, imitating and watching the parent. Jesus himself had learned his carpenter's/builder's trade from his father Joseph in that manner. Of course, a devoted parent would be most anxious to share everything with a child in regard to a lifelong career.

Jesus is so close to his Father and imitates him so completely that he can even do things usually reserved to God: raising the dead to new life and judging the world. This means that Jesus' word even now gives life to others, even to the dead. (We will see an example of this in Lazarus, chapter 11.) This releases every believer from fear of the future either at judgment (27) or at the general resurrection (29).

Witnesses to Jesus

5:30 **I can do nothing on my own.** Jesus does not push his own cause. He has the following witnesses who support his mission: 1) John the Baptist, **a burning and shining light** (35). 2) **The works** that God performs through him (36). 3) **The Father** who speaks within people, if they listen to his voice (37–38). 4) The scriptures that point to Jesus, especially those of Moses (39–47).

The Fourth Sign: The Multiplication of Bread

6:1 (See Mark 6:30–44; Matthew 14:13–21; Luke 9:10–17.) John, like Luke, has only one loaves' multiplication while Matthew and Mark have two. In addition, the first three gospels have a last supper institution account that John does not have in his own last supper story (13:1–38). This gospel has incorporated the meaning of Jesus' last supper in the long explanation that follows the feeding of the multitude. The feeding of the five thousand in John is the fourth and central of the seven great signs. It is central because all the other signs point to it. Just as John's gospel addresses differing views of Jesus' bread, so also it presents the various meanings of the bread that Jesus wished to be remembered by. The meaning of the bread corresponds to the meaning of his person and will be a principal means of his continued presence in the world.

A large crowd of sign-seekers (2) follows Jesus. John draws attention to the coming **Passover, the festival of the Jews**. The gospel will make a strong connection between Jesus' bread and the Passover meal. To show the inner power and nature of Jesus, the author highlights Jesus' foreknowledge and his definite plans. He takes the initiative in his concern for the crowd's hunger. He asks questions not really to obtain answers but as a test (5–6), since he knows what he is going to do. This foreknowledge of Jesus as the Word is characteristic of this gospel.

Only in John, a youth brings forward his own meager packed lunch to share with others. Likewise at the last supper it is the youthful beloved disciple who is at the bosom of Jesus. The theme of youth and renewal moves through the whole gospel. We note Jesus' careful supervision of everything about the meal including the seating, distribution and final gathering of fragments. It is the Lord's special banquet.

When the people saw the sign that he had done (14). The crowd's reaction is that Jesus' bread is one of power from a military as well as spiritual leader like Moses. This meaning of bread frightens Jesus who flees alone to the mountain to avoid the crowds who are eager to proclaim him as their king and messiah. The gospel audience then understands that Jesus' bread is not a "wonder bread" for superstar Christians. The mysterious night vision of Jesus walking on water signals a Passover motif. The Jews escaped Egypt and death by crossing the Red Sea. Jesus must also cross the waters of death in order to give his people the bread they need.

Jesus and the New Bread of Life

6:22 When the crowds finally locate Jesus, he tells them they have been searching for only the ordinary bread that fills the stomach: **You are looking for me, not because you saw**

signs but because you ate your fill of the loaves (26). In other
words, they have not perceived the sign value or deeper
meaning of what Jesus has done. Jesus' bread does not give
ordinary sustenance alone but **eternal life** (27). Jesus tells them
that this is the only bread they should work for. The people
naturally want to know how they can work for a bread of this
kind. However, only an interior work of faith and believing can
accomplish this: **This is the work of God, that you believe in
him whom he has sent** (29).

Yet the people still persist in looking for an external sign,
citing the biblical text, **He gave them bread from heaven to eat**
(Psalm 78:24). Jesus then begins to explain the nature of his
bread by beginning from this text. First he starts with a
summary: it is not a bread from Moses but from God, and **the
bread of God is that which comes down from heaven and
gives life to the world** (33). So it is a divine nourishment that can
sustain the whole world. The people ask, **Give us this bread
always** (34). This is an echo of the Lord's prayer petition which is
taken up by the audience.

Jesus then explains that he is the source of this bread for all
who come to him in discipleship: **I am the bread of life** (35). He
has come down from heaven with all that God has in order to
provide this bread of life. Jesus' goal is to bring everyone back to
God (in eternal life) by sharing his own eternal life as Word of
God in this bread. **Then the Jews began to complain**. Since there
are no non-Christian Jews in the gospel audience some sixty
years after Jesus' death, this refers to those Christians who still
limit Jesus to his earthly origins: **Is this not Jesus the son of
Joseph** (42)? Jesus replies that there is no external proof for his
teaching. Those who are close to God will recognize Jesus as
from God: **No one can come to me unless drawn by the Father
who sent me** (44).

Jesus moves to another level with his statement: **The bread
that I will give for the life of the world is my flesh** (51). While
the bread is truly divine, it is also completely human in
assimilating people to Jesus as human and divine. The word
flesh in the bible is used of human nature. However, Jesus will
be talking especially about the Passover meal where it is a matter
of "eating the flesh" of the Passover lamb (Exodus 12:8). This
statement of Jesus about eating his flesh like a sacrificial

Passover lamb prompts still others to object, **How can this man give us his flesh to eat?** (52).

Jesus replies very definitely, **Unless you eat the flesh of the Son of Man and drink his blood, you have no life in you**. For greater emphasis, this expression is repeated three times more in different terms in the next verses. If we substitute "body" for "flesh," we have the same expressions as in the last supper accounts of the synoptic gospels. There they are found in the context of Jesus' death and in a meal with Passover characteristics.

Putting together the Johannine special meaning of Jesus' bread, we obtain the following: it is a bread of discipleship made possible through faith. It is also a divine bread from heaven as well as a human, Passover sacrificial bread made possible by Jesus' death. Jesus' scriptural teaching concludes by a statement matching the opening one in 6:33: **This is the bread that came down from heaven** (58).

Jesus' Bread and the Words of Eternal Life

6:60 **This statement is difficult; who can accept it?** This verse shows that John's teaching on the eucharist is one that some Christians did not find it easy to accept. Jesus explains that only his death, resurrection, ascension and gift of the Spirit will make it possible. It cannot be understood in the literal expressions of "flesh" and "blood." **Many of his disciples turned back** (66). It is significant that Jesus turns to the twelve and that Peter and others support this new meaning of bread in this gospel. Since Peter was no longer alive when this gospel was written, it refers to Christians who are following a tradition of teaching coming from the apostle Peter.

PATHWAYS TO FURTHER DISCOVERY:

Trace the steps by which the Samaritan woman becomes a Christian leader in 4:1–42.

PERSONAL JOURNAL SUGGESTION:

Trace the various shades of meaning for Jesus' bread in John 6. What personal meaning does Jesus' bread have for you?

Jesus and the Feast of Tabernacles

7:1 The next great feast that Jesus fulfills is that of Booths or Tabernacles. Originally a joyful grape and fruit harvest, it was celebrated during September or October depending on the time of the full moon after the autumn equinox. During this harvest, many farmers made temporary dwellings or "booths" to remain near their crops and protect them.

The Jews added historical meanings to the festival. It became a feast commemorating their journey from Egypt to the promised land. During this time they moved from place to place living in tents while God accompanied them through his presence in the tent of the ark of the covenant. They remembered special signs of God's presence during this time. Among them was the miraculous water and bread God provided them in the desert to save their lives. Also, there was a fiery cloud that went before them night and day to show them the way. Even today, many Jews celebrate this feast by building temporary dwellings in their backyards where they eat, pray and meditate on the scriptures.

Jesus takes these themes of the feast and uses them to teach during the seven days of the festival. First, the journey theme as Jesus travels to Jerusalem and engages in dialogue about his continued presence as messiah. **Some people wonder, When the Messiah comes, no one will know where he is from** (27). Jesus replies that his origin indeed is mysterious from a Father they do not know (28–29). In connection with Jesus' journey and presence, we have predictions about his departure and return: for example, **I will be with you a little while longer and then I am going to him who sent me** (33). This statement is mysterious and misunderstood. They wonder if Jesus will go to the *diaspora*. These are the Jews scattered around the world due to various exiles. This is really ironical, for Jesus will go away in a local sense only to make his presence felt all over the world.

7:37 A second festal theme was that of miraculous water. To celebrate this there was a daily procession carrying water in golden jars from the pool of Siloam outside the city to the Jerusalem temple where it was poured on the altar. Jesus took up this theme on a dramatic occasion on the last of the seven festival days by announcing, **Let anyone who is thirsty come to me and**

drink. The evangelist takes special note of Jesus' statement, which he will remember at the foot of the cross through the sign of water flowing from Jesus' side (19:35). The phrase, **as yet there was no Spirit**, at first seems strange. However, the writer is thinking of the full, promised messianic Spirit that Jesus will give through his death and resurrection.

A Woman Caught in Adultery

8:1 This passage is not found here in most ancient Greek manuscripts. However, the passage fits nicely in with the judgment/decision motif of the feast; Jesus states in the next section: **You judge by human standards; I judge no one** (15).

Jesus the Light of the World

8:12 The Tabernacles feast themes continue. To commemorate God's guiding light in the desert, there was a spectacular outdoor lighting of the temple court. This could be seen many miles from Jerusalem as if a guiding beacon. As a new temple, Jesus declares, **I am the light of the world**. Those who follow this guiding light will never be in darkness but will be light-filled. He can be such a light because **I know where I came from and where I am going** (14).

Jesus Foretells His Death

8:21 The festival journey theme continues as Jesus says, **I am going away and you will search for me...where I am going you cannot come**. The reason they cannot come is that they are bound by the world's limitations (the meaning of "dying in one's sins" in verse 24). However, there is a way out: to believe that **I am he** (28). Here Jesus, as the eternal Word (1:1), plays on the meaning of God's own name revealed to Moses at the burning bush (Exodus 3:14). There, when Moses asked for God's name, God replied, "Tell them, 'I AM has sent me to you.'" However, Jesus can only show that he is this eternal **I AM** by going through death yet remaining alive: **When you have lifted up the Son of**

Man then you will realize that I am he (28). This picture of a continued presence and life that goes even beyond death is a source of courage for the audience as they face the future. Their own confidence can be the same as the conclusion of Jesus: **the one who sent me is with me; he has not left me alone.**

Disciples of Truth

8:31 **If you continue in my word...you will know the truth and the truth will make you free.** The same Greek lies behind English translations such as "continue," "stay," "abide," "remain," "dwell," and similar words. The indwelling theme of the festival continues. A sign of this will be the real truth which will be recognized by inner freedom. To explain this, Jesus cites the example of Abraham, their father, who traditionally had made them a free people. However, true freedom does not depend on any external ancestry or factors. It only comes from being released from the external bondage of sin.

Jesus and Abraham

8:39 A true child of God is not proved by ancestry but by imitation. Abraham was first and foremost one who believed and trusted in God as a Father. Those who are like Abraham are true children of God with love in their hearts for others. They cannot be "children of the devil," who prompted Cain to kill his brother out of hatred (Genesis 4:8).

Are we not right in saying that you are a Samaritan and have a devil? (48). Sincere believers, like Jesus, are often accused of being "fanatics." Yet they imitate Jesus in leaving the judgment to God. Jesus does not hold back because his teaching seems strange to others. He even states, **Whoever keeps my word will never see death** (52). This convinces some people that he indeed "has a devil," meaning that he is mad or a fanatic. The implication of Jesus' statement is that he is greater than all their religious founders before him. Abraham and all these people had looked forward to a future when God would dwell with his people as never before: **Your ancestor Abraham rejoiced that he would see my day** (in vision) (56).

Then Jesus makes his strongest statement to this point in John's gospel: **Before Abraham was, I AM**. Since Jesus is the creative Word of God, he can say this. **So they picked up stones to throw at him.** This sprinkling of stones was a customary response to words that hint blasphemy. This shows that he is close to deserving the blasphemy death punishment by stoning.

The Fifth Sign: Jesus Cures a Blind Man on the Sabbath

The fifth gospel sign is the curing of the man born blind. The story ending provides a key for the sign symbolism as Jesus states that he has come into the world so people can make choices and decisions: **that those who do not see may see, and those who do see may become blind** (39). This tells us that each of us in the gospel audience may identify with the blind man in his progress to obtain new vision.

All of us are **blind from birth**. We are limited by no one's fault to what we are capable of really seeing. Jesus comes as **the light of the world** (5) to cure this blindness. To accomplish this as a new creation, Jesus forms clay as God did in the beginning (Genesis 2:7). He then *anoints* (play of words on *messiah*, Anointed One) so we can see what we have never seen before. Before this can happen, we need new leadership and direction. So Jesus says, **Go to Siloam and wash** (7). The necessary response is to listen to his word and really *wash* through the waters of baptism: **He went and washed and came back able to see**. This step-by-step obedience enables us to accomplish the impossible.

Friends and people we know wonder if we are really the same helpless people, looking for hand-outs: **Is this not the man who used to sit and beg?** (8). Like the blind man, we keep answering "stupid questions" as to how it all happened. Even distinguished religion teachers (the Pharisees) interrogate us (13). With their great prestige, they cast doubts on the whole experience by saying that it was not done in the right way: This is because **it was a sabbath day when Jesus made the clay and opened his eyes** (14). The making of ointments was a prohibited sabbath day work according to religious law. The conclusion is that **this man is not from God for he does not observe the sabbath**.

There is a division among the people about the justification of such a work. The authorities ask the blind man for his opinion. A courageous step is to confront them by stating that Jesus is a prophet. Gradually we become no longer beggars but independent people, able to state our beliefs. The authorities try every means possible to look for ways to discount the miracle. Perhaps it was mistaken identification, so they call our parents to make a statement. They play it safe by saying that it indeed is true, but they do not know how he obtained new vision. Interestingly, they reply, **Ask him; he is of age. He will speak for himself** (23). In other words, our parents have been leading us, like blind people, through all the helpless years but now they can state that we are independent and mature, able to speak for ourselves—what a transformation!

His parents said this because they were afraid of the Jewish authorities who might expel them from the synagogue (22). This reflects the audience's situation near the end of the first century when they faced persecution for taking a stand on their belief in Jesus. Another interrogation follows to try to get us to weaken under pressure—the great method of all interrogators. Gradually we obtain new courage to face even our former teachers by demanding, **Why do you want to hear it again? Do you also want to become his disciples?** (28). This is a hint that our new insight has made us no longer passive students but even *teachers*.

Of course the learned professors emphasize their distinguished line of authority going back to Moses, **but as for this man, we do not know where he comes from** (29). We answer that this is just the point—that you do not know where he is from, yet like God at creation he opened my eyes. The learned teachers can only respond with a put-down that is ironically true: **You were born entirely in sin, and you are trying to teach us?**

The net result of this courageous stand is to be expected: **they drove him out**. This often happens when we see what others have never seen before and take the risk of expressing the truth to them. However, we are not left alone and abandoned (see 8:29). As the good shepherd in the next chapter, Jesus seeks out those who have been cast out. With his initiative the blind man (representing all of us readers) comes to full recognition of who Jesus is: he says, **"Lord, I believe." And he worshiped him**

(38). In recognition of the participatory nature of the blind man's story, it was the liturgical custom for many centuries for the whole congregation to stop at this point in the reading and kneel in worship together.

The final concluding paradox again brings out the representative role of the blind man. The Pharisees ask Jesus, **Surely we are not blind, are we?** Jesus answers them that the very insistence that they are not blind is the cause of failure to see. Only by admitting that we are blind can we make new vision a possibility.

PATHWAYS TO FURTHER DISCOVERY:

In comparison to the agricultural and historical meanings of the Jewish feast of Tabernacles, what new meanings does Jesus bring in?

PERSONAL JOURNAL SUGGESTION:

Imagine yourself in the scenes and dialogue of the blind man's story in chapter 9. As you identify with each person, what meanings do you find for yourself?

Jesus the Good Shepherd

10:1 The parables in this gospel differ from those in the synoptics. These latter deal with the nature of the kingdom of God, while those in John are concerned about relationship to Jesus. The audience context lies in the personal choices they must make to be true shepherds and leaders. Later we will see an example of this regarding Peter in 21:15–19. We will discover a contrast to the leadership of the Pharisees we have just observed in chapter 9 concerning the blind man's story.

The first image is that of a sheepfold. This is a low stone enclosure with a narrow gateway at one end. This is to enable a shepherd to safely guard the sheep, especially at night. The principal characteristic of a good shepherd is a personal relationship with each sheep: **the sheep hear his voice...he calls each of them by its own name...he goes ahead of them**.

Jesus draws this imagery of a good shepherd from God's own image given by the prophet Ezekiel. There God contrasts the approach of many human leaders to his own care and concern: **You eat the fat, you clothe yourselves with the wool, you slaughter the fatlings, but you do not feed the sheep** (34:3). John describes some shepherds/leaders as **thieves and bandits** (8) because they are mercenary and do not really care for the sheep. Later John will call Judas a thief because he looked out for his own interests rather than being a true leader (12:6).

The supreme quality of a good shepherd is the willingness to risk even one's life: **the good shepherd lays down his life for his sheep** (11), whereas others run away in the face of danger (12). Jesus' own relationship with people is so close that it is a mirror of his own relationship with God: **I know my own and my own know me, just as the Father knows me and I know the Father** (15). While John's gospel presents the highest level of understanding Jesus' person, it also has the highest divine understanding of the nature of discipleship.

I have other sheep that do not belong to this fold (16). The fourth gospel reaches out to those believers who do not have the same high levels of belief—they are still Jesus' sheep. The goal of Jesus is to bring all to a deep level of oneness—**one flock and one shepherd** (16). This oneness theme will be further developed in coming chapters. It is especially to create this oneness that Jesus says, **I lay down my life in order to take it up again**. Only John's gospel has Jesus raising himself up. The rest of the New Testament has God raising him up. John can write this because his gospel prologue states that the eternal Word is behind the humanity of Jesus. In addition, this gospel presents Jesus as both priest, the offerer, and the sacrifice that is offered—the new paschal lamb.

10:22 **The feast of Dedication**, called Hanukkah, occurs shortly before the Christmas season. It celebrates the rededication of the temple after it had been closed and desecrated by the Greeks for three years between 167 and 164 B.C. Like Jesus' death and resurrection, the temple could be closed and reopened because of the continuous presence of God that it celebrated. Likewise, no one can really take away Jesus' life. The eternal life he possesses is from the Father with whom he is intimately connected: **The Father and I are one** (30). Once again a reaction of token stoning takes place a second time (see 8:59) because of this daring statement.

Jesus tries to explain this statement by the custom of calling judges "gods" because God's word came through them. If this is so, how much more would "Son of God" accurately describe someone **God has sanctified and sent into the world** (36)? These words refer to the dedication (consecration) festival taking place at this time. Jesus can truly be called "Son of God," because he is God's temple on earth—expressed in the prologue with the words, **The Word became flesh and lived among us** (1:14).

Jesus makes a final appeal for belief in him at least because of the works (signs) that he does. **These show that the Father is in me and I am in the Father** (38). This bold statement again (see 7:44) provokes the authorities to arrest him. However, in this gospel no one can really *arrest* Jesus (nor a disciple) unless it is the *hour* when God allows it (see 18:1–11).

We might wonder why there is all this stress on Jesus' divinity in the fourth gospel. Certainly, development in Christology over the decades had much to do with it. This was enhanced by reflections on the Word/Wisdom of God in the wisdom biblical literature. God's personification of Wisdom in Proverbs 8–9 was especially important. However, there were two other important reasons. The first was to show Jewish Christians that believing in Jesus as God went far beyond their Jewish traditions. Yet much more important was the fact that Roman emperors increasingly proclaimed themselves as divine and all-powerful, requiring worship from all their subjects. It was necessary for Christians to understand that Christ was God, absolute Lord of the universe and far greater than any Roman emperor. This was especially necessary if Roman authority seemed superior by arresting and persecuting them. Above all, even if believers had to face death for their faith, they could trust that they would even overcome death and rise just as Jesus did by union with him as the Word and eternal life.

The Sixth Sign: The Raising of Lazarus

11:1 The Lazarus sequence includes most of chapter 11 and into chapter 12 and stands as a unit. The sign of the raising of Lazarus is the sixth gospel sign, although some scholars consider it as the seventh, counting the walking on water as one of them. The sign of Lazarus is really a sign of the resurrection of all believers, and the author is careful to bring in the audience at each step. In view of this, the Lazarus story has been told at Christian funerals for many centuries. It contains the typical questions asked at such funerals; for example, If Jesus can work miracles, why did he not help my beloved and work a cure?

Jesus receives a message from two disciples who are sisters: **Lord, he whom you love is ill.** They expect Jesus to immediately come and cure someone so close to him. The title, "One whom you love," is really the title of any believer. Martha and Mary are *beloved disciples as well:* Jesus loved **Martha and her sister**. The gospel is presenting a tragedy in a Christian family and showing the difference that believing in Jesus makes in such a situation.

Yet despite this urgent entreaty, Jesus delays and arrives too late to help the sick man. The perennial question is, "Why does Jesus delay in helping his beloved ones at the very time they need him most?" Jesus knows the question in the audience's mind and replies, **This illness does not lead to death; rather it is for God's glory.** In other words, there is no such thing as a *terminal* illness. Sometimes Jesus will cure through a miracle; at other times he delays only to work a greater miracle—a resurrection to a new life. This is the *glory* or manifestation of God's power.

Jesus then says to his disciples, **Let us go into Judea again** (7). The disciples are alarmed because Jesus had a narrow escape there recently when (in the last chapter) the crowd stoned him and the authorities tried to arrest him. However, Jesus' statement on being ready to return is especially significant: he will risk death (and ultimately does die) to raise Lazarus (and all believers) because they are *beloved disciples*. **Jesus replies, Are there not twelve hours of daylight?** In other words, God has established definite hours for day and night (life and death). Whatever happens is under God's power and plan. Jesus will only die when God's time has come.

Our friend Lazarus has fallen asleep, but I am going there to awaken him (11). The typical misunderstanding arises but Jesus means what he says—that death is like a temporary sleep from which Jesus awakens believers. Again Jesus says, **Let us go to him.** Thomas, the twin, understands that this means risking his own life as well and says to his fellow disciples, **Let us go that we may die with him** (16). Here there is a special play on the word "twin." Thomas is the model of a disciple who becomes a "twin" of Jesus in the sense of being ready to do what Jesus does, even repeating the same words as Jesus and being willing to die with him.

11:17 **He found that Lazarus had already been in the tomb four days.** For the audience to have hope, Lazarus must be literally rotting in the tomb like anyone else. This is repeated in verse 39 where Martha is concerned about the horrible stench of death if they open the tomb. Martha went out to meet Jesus and reproached him, **Lord, if you had been here, my brother would not have died** (21). In the biblical tradition, it is perfectly all right to complain to God; it is even a form of prayer. **But even now I know that God will give you whatever you ask of him.** Yet the ultimate in impossibility is death, so Jesus reassures her, **Your brother will rise again.** Martha responds with the typical traditional belief of most Jews that the resurrection will take place at the end of time.

In the fourth gospel view that the future is now (realized eschatology), Jesus replies, **I am the resurrection and the life** (25). This is because Jesus is the eternal Word and source of life for others (1:3–4). So he can add, **Those who believe in me, even though they die, will live.** Finally Jesus says to Martha (and the audience), **Do you believe this?** Martha responds, **Yes, Lord, I believe that you are the Christ, the Son of God.** Here Martha makes the great confession of faith that is reserved elsewhere to Peter (Matthew 16:16). She is the first one to do so in the gospel of John. Here as previously (chapter 4), a woman takes on a prominent role of leadership. She says these words at great risk since the authorities had warned that if any people confessed Jesus to be the Christ they should be thrown out of the synagogue (9:22).

11:28 The role of Mary, Martha's sister, is just as prominent, but in a non-verbal way. She just throws herself at Jesus' feet and can get no further than saying, **Lord, if you had been here my brother would not have died** before she breaks down in tears (32–33). Jesus is so moved that he begins to cry also. Jesus' humanity and feeling for others comes out stronger in this chapter than anywhere else in the gospel. Again, other people raise the same type of question as Martha, **Could not he who opened the eyes of a blind man have kept this man from dying?** (37).

11:38 Jesus faces the death of his friend Lazarus—and all his friends past and present—with every power of his being. He goes to the tomb and says, **Take away the stone.** This stone symbolizes the unremovable seal of death and all its powers. Martha and the others are terrified about all that this involves. But Jesus assures them as at the beginning (4), **Did I not tell you that if you believed you would behold the glory of God?** At this point we hear the prayer of Jesus as the majestic Word of God: **Father, I thank you for having heard me.** This is a continual prayer that is always answered for believers who die.

Then, with a loud voice, Jesus calls, **Lazarus, come out.** Jesus' call, that of the good shepherd—who also called Mary— (19), reaches even to a dead person who responds: **The dead person came out.** This action is a fulfillment and example of what Jesus had said for all: **The hour is coming and is now here, when the dead will hear the voice of the Son of God and those who hear will live** (5:25). The unbinding and loosening of the burial cloths further symbolizes the loosening of the bonds of death and true freedom from any fear of its power.

The Plot To Kill Jesus

11:45 The repercussions of the Lazarus miracles are quick and dramatic. Many people believe because of it. It prompts an urgent meeting of the chief priests and Pharisees. They are afraid to let Jesus continue on lest all believe in him as messiah and cause the Romans to take action. Caiaphas the high priest recommends the death penalty: **It is better for you to have one man die.** The author notes that Caiaphas made an unconscious prophecy that Jesus would die not only for the nation but for God's scattered children in the whole world. Jesus' death will not stop his work but expand it. Jesus withdraws from the Jerusalem area because the coming Passover feast will be his special time. The closing statement sets the stage for all that is to come: the authorities sent out orders **that anyone who knew where Jesus was should let them know, so they might arrest him.**

Mary Anoints Jesus at Bethany

12:1 The concluding arrest order in the previous section is a challenge for any believers facing possible arrest from authorities, Roman or otherwise, at any time. The Bethany community sets an example by refusing to comply. Instead, they put on a banquet in Jesus' honor for the signal gift of new life for their brother Lazarus. The events in chapter 12 are closely parallel to those of chapter 11. They are meant to be a response to Jesus' own risk of his life to save Lazarus and all beloved disciples.

There they gave a dinner for him. The Bethany house now becomes Jesus' home and model for the Christian family. As in the last chapter with her confession of faith, Martha takes the initiative by serving at table. Mary, as usual, expresses her response to Jesus in a non-verbal fashion. She performs the traditional hospitality role of washing Jesus' feet not just with water but with the most expensive ointment money could buy. She uses genuine **nard**, a word found only in the love poems of the Song of Songs. At Jesus' feet (as in 11:32) she then **wiped them with her hair.** This was a most affectionate and daring gesture that was quickly misunderstood by Judas. **The house was filled with the fragrance of the perfume.** This is a striking contrast to the odor of death in 11:39. Now the fragrance of the anointed body of Christ is at the center of the family and radiates outward.

Judas Iscariot, however, objected, **Why was this perfume not sold for three hundred denarii and the money given to the poor?** (5). Only John's gospel singles out Judas. Mary had responded to Jesus' act of love for Lazarus by great personal affection. In contrast, Judas thinks that a large donation for the poor would be more appropriate. The author notes that **he said this not because he cared for the poor**—this care and concern is the most important matter—**but because he was a thief.** In addition to money, the text has in mind those shepherds who do not really care for the sheep: **the thief comes only to steal and kill and destroy** (10:10). Jesus tells Judas to leave her alone. **She bought it so that she might keep it for the day of my burial.** Mary has recognized that Jesus faces death and burial because he has come to save Lazarus and others from death.

Jesus' Triumphal Entry into Jerusalem

12:9 The testimonial banquet of the courageous and affectionate Bethany community has wide repercussions. Others take courage because of their daring subversive action (in view of 11:57). First a great crowd comes to Bethany because of it. This also results in the authorities' plan to put to death Lazarus. Next, the Lazarus miracle and the Bethany response prompts a **great crowd** to accompany Jesus to Jerusalem: **They took branches of palm trees and went out to meet him**. The palms are only in John as a sign of triumph. Also he notes (as in 2:22) that **his disciples did not understand these things at first** (16). Only after Jesus' resurrection did they look back on these events and understand them in view of these scriptures. This shows that many events in Jesus' life are described from a post-resurrection viewpoint. As people read the Hebrew scriptures they found a new meaning in them with the help of the Holy Spirit. **Look, the whole world has gone after him** (19)! These words introduce the next passage as an ironic statement of the final effect of the Bethany "resistance" community.

Jesus' Coming Hour and Its World Effects

12:20 The Greek-speaking Jews who wish to see Jesus are a sign—the first-fruits of the whole world that will follow them. Hearing about these visitors, Jesus announces that **the hour has come** (23) to make the world harvest a reality. Jesus' death will be the seed dying in the earth to make that harvest possible. Following this, Jesus gives instructions for disciples who wish to follow the same way.

12:27 **Now my soul is troubled.** The gospel of John has no long prayer of Jesus in the garden of Gethsemane as do the other gospels. Instead we have the above "little agony" or relic of the garden scene that sums up the crisis of decision that Jesus faced. He will not pray to be saved from his terrible hour of suffering but only that his Father be glorified (by keeping his will). Jesus hears his Father's voice answering his prayer, but the people only hear what sounds like thunder. Then Jesus announces his decision: **Now is the judgment of this world; now the ruler of**

this world will be driven out (32). Thus, his death will be a final victory over all the evil powers in the universe. **When I am lifted up, I will draw all people to myself** (32).

This announcement of his death brings objections that the messiah, according to tradition, was to live forever. Jesus replies that he is indeed a light that never fades but it will be seen in his light-filled disciples. In this way the messiah will live on forever.

Conclusion of the Book of Signs (John 1–12)

12:36 **Although he had performed so many signs...they did not believe him.** This section is the conclusion of the book of signs. Rather we should say "imperfect signs." This is because the final sign will be on the cross with the water and blood flowing from Jesus' side. There is an atmosphere of sadness about all this, but Jesus says that it is not unexpected but typical of the vocation of a prophet. As an example, relatively few listened to God's message through Isaiah the prophet. John, however, notes that many, even from the authorities, believed in Jesus but kept their beliefs hidden out of fear. The final words in verses 44–50 are really a compendium of Jesus' sayings as a final conclusion of the book of signs.

PATHWAYS TO FURTHER DISCOVERY:

What actions and qualities of Martha and Mary in chapters 11 and 12 indicate that they are good models for women's leadership?

PERSONAL JOURNAL SUGGESTION:

Compare/contrast your own qualities as a shepherd/ leader with those of Jesus in 10:1–18.

JESUS' FINAL SUPPER, LAST WILL AND TESTAMENT, CHAPTERS 13-17

The opening mention of the Passover, Jesus' coming hour and his departure introduces Jesus' final supper and last discourse, chapters 13–17. They are Jesus' last will and testament to his disciples and the gospel audience. Jesus will reveal how his presence will continue and be recognized by them and the world. This will all be the result of Jesus' care for them as he looks to the future and provides for it: **He loved them to the end**.

13:1 The first action for continuity is the **washing of the disciples' feet**. There are two aspects of this. The first concerns *how* Jesus can do what he has in mind. This will be with the complete divine power the Father has given him: **knowing the Father had given all things into his hands**. At the same time it will be in his full humanity as a humble servant of God. The details seem symbolic—laying aside the outer garment of nobility (the privileges of divinity) and assuming the garb of a slave (his humanity) in the most humble activity possible. Often slaves washed the soiled feet of those coming in from streets, feet soiled with dirt and animal dung.

The second aspect is the meaning of what Jesus is actually doing—something that the audience will also be able to do (13–16). Jesus performs the ordinary ritual of hospitality. This involves cleansing dirty feet and accepting guests into the home with all the privileges of the family circle. However, Jesus' acceptance goes even deeper since it includes full forgiveness of anything that would impede full family union in his Father's house.

Peter does not understand this total meaning and will not accept Jesus' humiliation (ultimately the cross) to make it possible. But Jesus tells him that he must do so to have a complete share in Jesus' work. Peter answers, **Lord, not my feet only, but also my hands and head** (9). Jesus replies that he has indeed been bathed/cleansed—a message to the audience about their total baptismal cleansing. However, they and also Peter need a partial foot cleansing. This symbolizes the everyday "dirt of the road," sins and transgressions that must be forgiven.

After Jesus puts back on the outer garment, he tells his disciples that they are to continue the same loving ministry: **If I, your Lord and teacher, have washed your feet, you also ought to wash one another's feet** (14). In the total gospel context, in view of the coming feast of Passover (1), Jesus will be **the Lamb of God who takes away the sin of the world** (1:29). Only he can effect this total once-and-for-all cleansing. *Sin* of the world is singular—referring to closure to relationship and faith. However, Jesus will convey to his disciples the power to forgive *sins* (plural), the daily transgressions. This will be done on Easter Sunday evening when he breathes on them, gives them the Holy Spirit and says, **If you forgive the sins of any, they are forgiven them** (20:23).

Jesus Foretells His Betrayal

13:21 The next great sign of Jesus' love "to the end" occurs during the betrayal of Judas. This will not be an unforeseen tragedy. Jesus knows it will happen. He is even deeply **troubled in spirit** as he announces to the group that one of them will betray him. Yet despite this, Jesus goes ahead. He even shows Judas a special sign of love by personally giving him a choice morsel from the common platter and talking to him to show that he does know. No one else even suspected Judas. He had a trusted community responsibility in taking care of the common purse and making purchases.

One of his disciples, the one whom Jesus loved, was reclining next to him (23). This disciple has a prominent place at Jesus' last supper. Literally, he was reclining "at his bosom," meaning at his right side of honor since people at table reclined on their left elbow with their feet pointing outward. This beloved disciple is at Jesus' bosom just as Jesus is in the bosom of the Father (1:18). Thus he is the revealer of Jesus, just as Jesus reveals the Father. This disciple is not only the ideal disciple, representing the audience, but a source of this gospel, a prominent witness of Jesus' death and a special successor as well (19:25–27; 20:2–8). His role at the last supper is unusual and symbolizes his teaching office: he is the first to share Jesus' great secret about the identity of his betrayer. Even Peter asks him to find out who the betrayer is. Thus the beloved disciple is like an "inner successor" of Jesus, while Peter is like the "outer successor."

Judas leaves the table at the symbolic time of darkness since Satan, the prince of darkness, **entered into him** (27). This sets in motion all the forces that will lead to Jesus' death so Jesus will say, **Now the Son of Man has been glorified**. Jesus will go away from exterior sight but furnishes a sign for recognizing his interior presence: **I give you a new commandment, that you**

love one another (34). The new element is the special quality of this love. It is a love for even a betrayer like Judas. This type of love will show people how to find disciples of Jesus: **By this everyone will know that you are my disciples**.

13:36 Jesus' command of love becomes even more unusual as we see him going ahead even knowing that his principal leader, Peter, will fail also. The gospel ending will show how Peter recovers and learns to be a good shepherd by laying down his life like Jesus.

Jesus' Last Discourse and Final Testament, 14–17

14:1 Chapters 14–17 continue the last supper scene. Jesus is going away and leaves his last instructions and overview of the future. As in the synoptic gospels, the *parousia* or return of Jesus is very definite. However, there is no coming of the Son of Man in the clouds like the other gospels. Instead, the *parousia* becomes an on-going process leading to a culminating point in the future. John will concentrate on the signs of the presence of the risen Jesus in the community listening to the gospel reading.

In these chapters, there will be much repetition for added stress and memory but never word for word; there will always be an added element. Thomas the twin wants to know the way to follow Jesus, but this consists first in knowing Jesus. This is already arriving close to the destination: **I am the way and the truth and the life** (6). Philip wants something more demonstrative, but it will only come through the relationship of believing: **Do you not believe that I am in the Father and the Father is in me?** (10). This *believing* will be the root of various ways of knowing the Father. It will result in **greater works than these** (12) as disciples duplicate and spread the works of the master.

Finally, a close inner relationship with Jesus will result in a communion of prayer so close that their prayer will be as powerful as that of Jesus: **I will do whatever you ask in my name** (13). "In Jesus' name" means because of him, and united to him.

The Promise of the Holy Spirit

14:15 The greatest sign of God's presence will be the gift of the Holy Spirit that Jesus will confer on the Sunday night of his resurrection (20:22). Jesus will ask the Father and he will send **another advocate to be with you forever**. The word "Advocate," literally, *parakletos*, means one who acts for another with all that person's power—something like "power of attorney" today. The text reads **another advocate**, because Jesus is the first in relationship to his Father. The "second advocate" duplicates all that Jesus does, acting as if a "twin" of Jesus.

The images of God's presence flow freely from one to another. For example, Jesus then says in the first person, **I will not leave you orphaned; I am coming to you** (18). How will this happen? It is through the strongest statement of identification with Jesus that is found in the gospel: **On that day you will know that I am in the Father and you in me and I in you** (20). The mention of "on that day" makes Judas (not the Iscariot) think in terms of a glorious future triumphant return. However Jesus warns that this return will be more interior than exterior. It will be an inner witness and presence that will be manifested in keeping his words (23).

A second promise of the Spirit follows, but now it is the **Advocate, the Holy Spirit...who will teach you everything** (25). Here specifically, the Spirit, acting in disciples, duplicates Jesus' work. Jesus was a teacher and now the Spirit in believers is a teacher reminding people of Jesus' words. We note that the Spirit as teacher in this gospel is the essential inner successor of Jesus, whereas Matthew stressed the role of Peter as outer successor and teacher (16:16–20). This gift of the Spirit is closely connected to peace: **Peace I leave with you** (27). This gift of peace is linked to forgiveness and reconciliation. Jesus will connect together peace and forgiveness on the first Sunday night after his resurrection (20:19–23).

Jesus declares that they should rejoice that he is returning to the Father because **the Father is greater than I am** (28). This is a strong statement of Jesus' humanity. The Arian heresy in the fourth century used this text to claim a dependence of Jesus on the Father. However, the Council of Nicea in 325, in condemning Arius, went to the other extreme of almost submerging Jesus in a doctrine of the Trinity. This led to losing appreciation of Jesus' humanity as one with his people as well as mediator.

The ending of chapter 14, **Rise, let us be on our way,** may indicate an original ending of the discourse. If so, the following chapters were later added as an afterthought by the author or others.

Jesus the True Vine: Union and Opposition

15:1 The images of vine and vineyard are familiar biblical references to God and his people from Isaiah 5:1–7. The "pruning" is part of God's loving care that God exerts on his people through Jesus. The whole image of a branch bearing fruit points to Jesus' abiding presence that produces the "fruit" of additional believers. **I am the vine and you are the branches. Those who abide in me** (5). This inner abiding presence is essential, for **without me you can do nothing.** A sign of this inner presence (second mention, with a third in verse 16) will be prayer: **Ask for whatever you wish and it will be done for you.**

Another sign of Jesus' Spirit/presence will be a new kind of love, like that of Jesus—**that you love one another as I have loved you** (12). A first quality makes it similar to that of Jesus in being willing to risk one's life: **to lay down one's life for one's friends** (13). A second quality is a love based on equality: **I have called you friends** (15). A third quality is initiative and risk: **You did not choose me but I chose you.** Most students then as now choose their own teachers. Instead, Jesus chose his own disciples as a model for action.

The next sign of Jesus' presence will be especially difficult to accept: **If the world hates you, be aware that it hated me before you** (18). Disciples are not to take this personally; it will only show that they do not serve the "world" as Jesus did not. This links with another description of the Advocate who will **testify on my behalf, and you also are to testify** (26). The word "testify" is from the Greek root **martyr** from which the verb used here is taken. Witnesses make the greatest impression when they do so at the risk of life.

The author spends much time on this question of persecution. It comes from two sources. The first is the synagogue where

Jewish Christians may find themselves rejected by even family and close friends (for example the blind man in 9:22, 34). However, much more dangerous, widespread and life-threatening was Roman persecution where **those who kill you will think that by doing so they are offering worship to God** (16:2). The Romans often called Christians "atheists" because they did not believe that the daily religious/civil sacrifices to the gods were necessary. This was especially the case when Christians did not recognize and bow down before Roman "divine" emperors who claimed godlike status and demanded worship from the people.

The Work of the Spirit Coming After Jesus' Departure

16:5 We now have more descriptions of the Spirit/Paraclete as continuing Jesus' work. Jesus as a prophet had put the world on trial and the world had seemed to win upon Jesus' death. However, all will be reversed: the Spirit as Advocate/prosecuting attorney will show that the world was wrong in three areas. 1) Regarding sin—that Jesus was not guilty of sin but that the world had the basic sin in lack of openness or believing in him. 2) Regarding righteousness—they will find that the one whom they condemned is now the one who establishes justice and righteousness. 3) Regarding judgment—that Satan who thought he had triumphed and judged the world is now judged and overcome by God through Jesus.

When the Spirit of truth comes, he will guide you into all the truth (13). Jesus had said that he was the truth (14:6). Now the Spirit as double of Jesus will continue this work in new generations. This is the source of the gospel of John which has a new word of Jesus to a new generation of believers. The Spirit will also open up the meaning of the future as well.

Temporary Sorrow Followed by Joy

16:16 The farewell discourse moves toward conclusion on the themes of temporary sorrow on Jesus' departure along with permanent interior joy: **You will weep and lament but the world will rejoice** (20). Jesus warns the audience that they will face temporary sorrow as they appear to the world to be "losers," while opponents seem to be joyful "winners." The birth of a new age will have its own birthpangs like those of a woman in childbirth (21). The words "joy" or "rejoice" are repeated five times in this chapter. Joy is Jesus' parting gift. It will be experienced especially in prayer that is always answered: **Ask and you will receive that your joy may be complete** (24).

To conclude his final discourse, Jesus speaks openly of himself as the Word of God and returns to the same opening words of 13:1 about coming from the Father and returning again (28). The disciples affirm their belief, but Jesus tells them that believing is only certified by the willingness to face opposition. So the question **Do you now believe?** (31) is really addressed to the gospel audience. When they are scattered, alone, and without Jesus' physical presence, this will be the real test. However, Jesus' source of confidence will be their own as well: **I am not alone, because the Father is with me** (32). Jesus' final words and source of courage are: **Take courage; I have conquered the world.**

Jesus' Final Priestly Prayer

17:1 At this point in the other gospels, we had Jesus' agonizing prayer in the Garden of Olives before his arrest. However, the atmosphere here is quite distinct. Jesus' prayer is for his disciples and audience rather than for himself. Jesus has already conquered (16:33) and is on the verge of returning in triumph to his Father. At this long awaited hour, Jesus is like an eternal high priest assuring his disciples about the future by his continual, all-powerful prayer. This is because God has given him **authority over all people to give eternal life to all whom you have given him** (2).

Jesus has given his disciples everything he has received from the Father—his name is their name also (6). His great prayer to his Father is **that they may be one even as we are** (11). Jesus' prayer has some similarities to the Lord's prayer in asking that they be protected from the evil one (15) and sanctified in the truth (17). The words "sanctify" and "consecrate" refer to the coming gift of his own life. He asks that his disciples may be able to do the same if called upon.

Jesus' prayer even goes out to the future **to those who will believe in me through their word** (20). A sign to the world will be the continued oneness of believers: **As you, Father, are in me and I am in you, may they also be one in us that the world may believe that you have sent me.** This is repeated in the next verse to stress its importance. This oneness will be witnessed in their love for one another that will manifest God's own love to the world. So the final testament and prayer of Jesus concludes with the beautiful words: **that the love with which you have loved me may be in them, and I in them.**

PATHWAYS TO FURTHER DISCOVERY:

After rereading chapters 14 to 16, list the ways that the Advocate/Holy Spirit may be found in the world today.

PERSONAL JOURNAL SUGGESTION:

The Paraclete/Holy Spirit is Jesus' inner successor. In what ways do you find the Spirit at work in your own life?

The Arrest of Jesus

18:1 Jesus' arrest in John has a unique dramatic atmosphere. It is meant to give courage to anyone in the audience facing opposition or arrest from any power. These powers are represented by the three groups that come to arrest Jesus. First, Judas stands for the prince of darkness who had entered into him at the last supper (13:2). Second, the police represent the Jewish authorities. Finally, the soldiers symbolize all the powers of the Roman empire. Jesus, however, is in full control—**knowing all that was to happen to him** (4). He even takes the initiative, steps forward and asks, **Whom are you looking for?**

What follows is really the effect of Jesus' previous prayer that the divine name protect his disciples (17:11). When Jesus replies **I AM (he)**, he is really pronouncing the great revelation name of God ("I AM") revealed to Moses at the burning bush (Exodus 3:14). At the power of this name, all the hostile powers of the world **stepped back and fell to the ground** (6). These last words are a symbolic biblical expression for complete defeat. The whole sequence is repeated to stress its certainty. On the third attempt, Jesus willingly hands himself over. This proves that no earthly power can possibly arrest him or his disciples without divine permission. So Jesus says, **If you are looking for me, let these men go** (8). Thus Jesus gives his own life, as he did for Lazarus, that they may be free. As Jesus promised in his last prayer, he will never lose anyone who believes in him (18:9).

The High Priest Questions Jesus and Peter's Denial

18:12 Only John has a special appearance of Jesus before the high priest Annas. The scope of questioning is about Jesus' disciples and teachings. The high priest is looking for a pretext to denounce Jesus to Roman power as a political revolutionary. Jesus' teaching, however, has been open and public, not secret, in order to enlist followers for a revolution. The gospel suggests that Jesus is the real high priest placing Annas on trial by demanding reasons for his accusations and ill treatment.

18:15 For Peter's denial, see Mark 14:66–72. In John's gospel, Peter's behavior is contrasted to that of "the other disciple," the beloved disciple of 13:23. This disciple faithfully followed Jesus even after his arrest. The evangelist draws a dramatic contrast between Jesus' statement before his arrest and Peter's. Jesus had responded "I AM" to the arresters' questioning; Peter replied "I AM NOT" (18:25). This tells the audience that failure to bear the divine name and trust in it will lead to failure.

Jesus Before Pilate

18:28 (See Mark 15:1–15.) John will keep mentioning the **Passover** (18:28, 34; 19:14) to remind us that Jesus is being led toward death at the same time that the Passover lambs were prepared for sacrifice and the Passover meal that began after sunset. Like the synoptics, Pilate proclaims Jesus' innocence repeatedly. Unique to John are the personal exchanges with Pilate inside the praetorium. The first one concerns the charge that Jesus is the **king of the Jews** (33). Jesus replies, **My kingdom is not from this world**. From what follows, this means that he is not like kings who rely on force and power. Jesus acknowledges that he is indeed a king who has come into the world to witness to the truth. True followers will listen to his voice. Pilate, of course, will not, so he replies, "What is truth?"

Pilate Sentences Jesus to Death

19:1 (See Mark 15:15–20.) Only John has Pilate publicly present Jesus to the crowd with a **crown of thorns** and dressed in a **purple robe** (19:2), mentioned again for emphasis in verse 5. This is the well-known tableau painted by famous artists entitled *Ecce Homo*, **Behold the Man** (5). The evangelist wants the audience to see Jesus in the way he is truly king—as a crucified messiah. This is an appeal for a decision of repentance and love, for it is the way that Jesus will draw the world to himself (12:32–33).

After Pilate's third declaration of Jesus' innocence (6) of political charges, the Jewish authorities present a religious charge: that Jesus was guilty of blasphemy by claiming to be Son of God. Actually, only John's gospel has explicit statements of Jesus or others that he is God (e.g. 10:30). These statements occur in a gospel written many years after Jesus' death and represent a gradual development in understanding Jesus' person. At the time the gospel was written, Jews would regard such statements as blasphemous and worthy of death according to biblical laws.

This religious accusation frightens Pilate and results in more dialogue inside. Pilate wants to know Jesus' real origin, asking **Where are you from?** When Pilate persists, Jesus responds that the governor has no power over him (or the audience) unless given to him from above by God. The final judgment scene before the people is carefully described. Many in the audience will face such judgments in government tribunals. Jesus is the real judge, not Pilate. Will they choose a humiliated, crucified messiah or will they, like Pilate and his puppets, say, **We have no king but Caesar** (15)?

The Crucifixion of Jesus

19:16 Many details of the synoptics are missing but John includes others with special new meanings. **Carrying the cross for himself.** There is no Simon of Cyrene to help him. Jesus is a confident figure carrying the cross alone. The Johannine passion account is much more a triumphant story than the other gospels. The cross inscription receives special attention as a proclamation to the whole world about God's crucified messiah and king. The world is symbolized by the three languages—**Hebrew, Latin and Greek** (20). This proclamation form is troublesome to the Jewish authorities who only want it specified that Jesus made that claim. Pilate, previously so vacillating, refuses to change it. This hints that the proclamation is God's plan.

The soldiers divide Jesus' garments into **four parts**. The number *four* in the bible has a universal thrust and symbolizes the universal effect of Jesus' death. Jesus' tunic also receives special attention. The **tunic was seamless, woven in one piece** (23), so the soldiers did not wish to tear it. This follows the universal emphasis and suggests the theme of oneness despite increasing numbers (as in 21:11). It is also possible that the seamless tunic represents the long tunic of the high priest, since Jesus as priest offers himself as the paschal lamb sacrifice for the sins of the world (1:29).

The Mother of Jesus and the Beloved Disciple

19:25b Only the fourth gospel has the mother of Jesus present at the cross as she was at Jesus' first miracle at Cana. There, Jesus had spoken of his hour to come when his mother's request would have full meaning (2:4). The group at the cross is a special witness both of the reality of Jesus' death and the unusual way that he died. Also, there is an important teaching on succession and the credentials of the gospel author. The beloved disciple, source of the gospel, is at Jesus' side at his great hour and takes Jesus' place in his family as an adopted son. This confers special authority on the gospel and its teaching. Also, as ideal adopted son, the audience becomes part of Jesus' own family through his death on the cross.

The Death of Jesus

19:28 **After this, when Jesus knew that all was finished** (28). Jesus, as divine Word, is in supreme control as to when and how he will die. It is a voluntary death as he offers himself to the Father. To fulfill God's plan, he says, **I thirst**, quoting from Psalm 69:21, which reads, **In my thirst they gave me (sour) wine to drink.** Jesus then takes some of the wine offered him to conform with God's plan in the scriptures. Here we note a connection to the wedding at Cana in chapter 2: Jesus takes the cup of wine (suffering) from his Father at the cross, obedient as far as death; at Cana, Jesus' mother asks for obedience to Jesus to make possible the new wine at Cana. Jesus can now deliberately say, **It is finished**, because he has done all that his Father has asked of him. The symbolism of the wine at Cana becomes stronger when we note that the Semitic expression for wine is "the blood of the grape."

Then he bowed his head and gave up his spirit. This phrase hints that he breathed out his Spirit and gave it to others (see 20:22). This is especially significant for the beloved disciple by the cross since he represents the ideal believer and example of one guided by the Spirit.

The Seventh Sign: The Piercing of Jesus' Side

19:31 The essential witnesses are already present for the seventh and final great sign of the gospel. This is the **blood and water** that flowed from Jesus' side after a soldier **pierced his side with a spear**. The gospel writer tells the audience that this has special meaning for them: **He who saw this has testified so that you also may believe** (35). The flowing blood fulfills a requirement for the paschal lamb sacrifice that blood should actually flow. It also refers to God's sign of salvation to the people in the first Passover in Egypt: **The blood shall be a sign for you on the houses where you live. When I see the blood, I will pass over you** (Exodus 12:13).

The water from Jesus' side is also a sign of the Spirit since it reminds the audience of Jesus' promise at the Tabernacles feast to give living water: **Out of him shall flow fountains of living water** (7:38–39). It is also a reminder of God's promise in Ezekiel that a fountain of living water would arise from under the temple altar in the new age. This source would become a flowing river, widening and deepening until it turns the Dead

Sea into a new Garden of Eden (47:1–12).

Other scriptures complete the pattern of God's plan. The fact that the soldiers did not break any of Jesus' bones recalls the Passover ritual requirement for the lamb: **None of his bones shall be broken** (36; Exodus 12:46). The "seeing" of the blood of the Passover lamb, mentioned above, was essential to the sign of the first Passover. This looking and seeing motif continues as the beloved disciple and the women look on (35). This prompts another scripture reference: **They look on the one whom they have pierced** (Zechariah 12:10). The result of this will be (as the verse continues) that **I (God) will pour out a spirit of compassion and supplication on the house of David**.

This sign of the paschal lamb's blood completes and fulfills the Baptist's introduction of Jesus to the first disciples: **Here is the lamb of God who takes away the sin of the world** (1:29, 35). Thus, the beginning and end of the gospel come together. Jesus is not only the paschal lamb; he is also, as eternal Word, the eternal priest who offers this sacrifice up to God (10:18).

The Burial of Jesus

19:38 The burial scene points to some first fruits of those whom Jesus draws to himself through the cross (12:32). Secret disciples like Nicodemus and Joseph of Arimathea come into the open and risk persecution to bury the body of Jesus. This encourages secret disciples among the audience to also come out and dare to confess what they really believe. The **hundred pounds** of **myrrh and aloes**, not mentioned elsewhere, is most unusual and extravagant. Perhaps it symbolizes the royal triumphant burial of a messiah who has undergone the disgrace and humiliation of the cross. The triple mention of a garden (19:41; 20:15) evokes, as in Luke, the image of a restored Garden of Eden and human family.

The Resurrection of Jesus

20:1 Mary Magdalene, rising early to go to the tomb, finds it empty and runs to tell the two disciples who then run together toward the tomb. The story focuses on the experience of the beloved disciple. It is enough to see the empty tomb and the burial garments for him to believe that Jesus has risen. This is a model for every "beloved disciple" who needs no further proof. Both disciples then await the further proof of the Spirit who will reveal to them that the death and resurrection of the messiah is part of God's plan in the scriptures.

Jesus First Appears to Mary Magdalene

20:11 Mary Magdalene is now the central figure as an audience model of one who keeps searching intensively for Jesus. Four times her weeping is mentioned (11, 13, 15). Yet she does not recognize Jesus when she sees him, and thinks he is the gardener (16). This is because of Jesus' transformed resurrection body. Only when Jesus calls her does she turn (also in a deeper sense) and recognize him. John had already written that the sheep recognize the voice of a true shepherd (10:4). Mary responds with a term of endearment **Rabboni! (which means teacher)**.

Jesus then entrusts to Mary a special mission, that of being an apostle to the apostles (17). Thus she completes the series of examples of women's leadership that are unique to this gospel. Her mission is to tell the disciples that Jesus is ascending (returning) to the Father. This of course cannot be seen by human eyes, but will be symbolized when Jesus gives them the Holy Spirit from his Father. Jesus has never before said, "My Father and *your Father*." Now, however, his disciples can say this in the same way that Jesus has said it.

Jesus' Final Commission and Gift of the Spirit

20:19 Mary Magdalene's special announcement prepares the way for Jesus' final commission to his disciples and the gift of the Holy Spirit. The scene is not meant to be ancient history but a typical community gathering when this experience is repeated. The community gathers on the **first day of the week** (Sunday). It does not matter if **doors of the house are locked** because the community has to risk danger if they meet together. Jesus suddenly appears and greets people then and always with the words, **Peace be with you**. The believers can recognize that it is the same crucified Jesus because of the marks of the crucifixion on his hands and his side.

Just as Jesus went out to the world with the presence and power of God, so also the community shares the same mission: **As the Father has sent me, I also send you**. To guarantee this identification with himself, Jesus breathes upon them and says, **Receive the Holy Spirit**. The author describes Jesus' breathing action with the same Greek verb as Genesis 2:7. There God created the first human being and **breathed into his nostrils the breath of life**. Spirit and breath come from the same root word. Jesus' action is like a new creation and symbolizes the special gift of his own inner Spirit to his disciples and audience. This Spirit will be especially manifest in the ministry of forgiveness— so much so that the community's acceptance and forgiveness will be that of God: **If you forgive the sins of any, they are forgiven them**.

Jesus and Thomas the Twin

20:24 This incident has even entered the English dictionary with the phrase, "a doubting Thomas," a person who does not believe unless given physical proof. Thomas wants that kind of proof and will not accept the testimony of others who tell him, **We have seen the Lord**. However, Thomas does come to the community gathering a week later on Sunday. This already implies a change in his attitude. Jesus appears in their midst again and reproachfully invites Thomas to obtain his "proof" by examining his nail wounds and side.

However, Thomas does not do so but exclaims, **My Lord and my God!** These are words of pure faith and are a title for God alone used in Psalm 35:23. This declaration is the climax of the great Johannine journey which began in 1:51 with Jesus' prediction that the disciples would see the heavens opened to reveal who Jesus is. The first gospel verse had stated that the **Word was God**, and now the concluding journey statement affirms this of the risen Jesus.

After this, we have a conclusion addressed to both Thomas and the audience: Jesus says, **Have you believed because you**

have seen me? Then Jesus confers a final blessing on the gospel audience, who like the beloved disciple at the tomb have believed without physical proofs: **Blessed are those who have not seen and yet have come to believe.**

Conclusion and Author's Purpose

20:30 The author now writes his own conclusion, stating the purpose of his gospel. Over a hundred times the verb **believe** has appeared in the gospel. It has denoted a deep personal trust and relationship. The result of this will be sharing the same **life** as that of Jesus described in the gospel opening: **In him was life.**

The above section seems to have been an original ending of the gospel. At some time before its publication, chapter 21 was added either by the author or by someone else and became part of the gospel. The following are some reasons for this addition. Chapter 21 emphasizes the role of Peter as leader and shepherd. This seems a balance to the rest of the gospel where the beloved disciple is more prominent. Also, the apparitions in this chapter belong to a Galilee collection of stories (like those in Matthew) and would thus supplement the Jerusalem accounts in chapter 20. At any event, they have been carefully interwoven with the rest of the gospel and furnish valuable additional testimonies.

EPILOGUE AND APPENDIX, CHAPTER 21

The apparitions in chapter 21 are for teaching purposes and point to additional ways that Jesus' presence and power will be recognized. The first is Peter's mysterious fishing expedition. It resembles the story in Luke 5:1–11 where it occurs in Jesus' earthly life. As in Luke, the apostles work all night and catch nothing, but at Jesus' command, the net becomes filled with large fish, **a hundred fifty-three of them** (11). Exegetes have sought the meaning of this number for almost two thousand years. Letters of the Greek and Hebrew alphabet can also stand for numbers, so this gives ample opportunity for detective work. Back in the fourth century, St. Jerome suggested that there were 153 varieties of fish! Perhaps the number signifies fish of every kind—a symbol of a great variety of human beings from all over the world. At any rate, this first sign tells us that when the "big fish" come in during a successful apostolate directed by Peter, then this is a sure sign of the master's presence.

A second sign of Jesus' presence will be during community meals (9–13) prepared by Jesus himself. Jesus will thus continue his role as nourishing shepherd, but we note that he does so with the cooperation of Peter and the apostles. The writer draws attention to the fact that **the net was not torn** (11) despite the enormous quantity of large fish of every kind. Here again we have the Johannine oneness theme to bring out that the community is still united as they share meals together despite the number and diversity of converts. It is interesting that in the two connected stories, the beloved disciple (7) and Peter have complementary roles. Peter directs the outer apostolate, while the other disciple is the revealer of Jesus' inner presence.

21:15 A third sign will be the shepherding role of Jesus as carried on by Peter and other shepherds after him. Peter had boasted he would never abandon his master, even if he had to give his life (13:36–38). Yet despite this boast, he gave in to human weakness and denied Jesus three times. For this reason, Jesus asks Peter three times, **Simon, son of John, do you love me?** Each time, Jesus responds, **Feed my lambs/sheep**. The real proof of Peter's love will be his care and feeding of Jesus' own sheep.

However, a good shepherd, like Jesus, is one who lays down his life for his sheep (10:11). So Jesus predicts (as in 13:36) that Peter will be led to his death on a cross in the same way as his master (18–19). A death on a cross seems indicated because of the description and because the same phrase is used in Jesus' own prediction of his death in 12:33. By the time the gospel was written (toward the beginning of the second century), Peter had already become a martyr in Rome in the early 60s. His example is important for those in the audience called upon to risk their lives as good shepherds.

21:20 A final story about the beloved disciple was meant to correct the impression that Jesus had predicted that he would remain alive until Jesus' second coming. A postscript (24) certifies that it is indeed this beloved disciple who is the source of this gospel. A second postscript (25) appears to have been added by a transcriber of the gospel or another writer. The first person "I" is never used elsewhere by the gospel writer.

PATHWAYS TO FURTHER DISCOVERY:

Glance again through the stories of the passion of Jesus in Mark, Matthew and Luke. In comparison, what distinctive characteristics do the corresponding Johannine stories have?

PERSONAL JOURNAL SUGGESTION:

Read again the story of Mary Magdalene in John 20. What possible symbolic meaning does it have for you concerning a personal search for Jesus?

Some Additional
Recommended Readings

For Study of Gospel Parallels:

Gospel Parallels (New York: Nelson, 1971)
New Gospel Parallels, ed. Robert Funk, 2 vols. (Philadelphia: Fortress, 1985)

For the Gospel of Mark:

Fowler, Robert M., *Let the Reader Understand* (Minneapolis: Augsburg Fortress, 1991)
Harrington, Wilfred, *Mark* (Wilmington: Michael Glazier, 1979)
Heil, John Paul, *The Gospel of Mark as Model for Action: A Reader-Response Commentary* (Mahwah: Paulist Press, 1992)
Robbins, Vernon, *Jesus the Teacher, A Socio-Rhetorical Interpretation of Mark* (Philadelphia: Fortress, 1984)

For the Gospel of Matthew:

Gundry, Robert H., *Matthew: A Commentary on His Handbook for a Mixed Church under Persecution* (Grand Rapids: Eerdmans, 1994 rev. ed.)
Harrington, Daniel, *The Gospel of Matthew* (Collegeville: Liturgical Press, 1991)
Kingsbury, Jack Dean, *Matthew as Story* (Minneapolis: Augsburg Fortress, 1988)
Meier, John P., *Matthew* (Wilmington: Michael Glazier, 1981)

217

For the Gospel of Luke:

Ellis, E. Earle, *Luke* (Grand Rapids: Eerdmans, 1981)

Fitzmyer, Joseph, *The Gospel According to Luke* (Garden City: Doubleday, 1981)

Johnson, Luke Timothy, *The Gospel of Luke* (Collegeville: Liturgical Press,1991)

LaVerdiere, Eugene, *Luke* (Wilmington: Michael Glazier, 1980)

For the Gospel of John:

Brown, Raymond E., *The Gospel and Epistles of John: A Concise Commentary* (Collegeville: Liturgical Press, 1988)

_____ *The Community of the Beloved Disciple* (Ramsey: Paulist Press, 1979)

Culpepper, R. Alan, *Anatomy of the Fourth Gospel: A Study of Literary Design* (Philadelphia: Fortress, 1994 rev. ed.)

Grassi, Joseph A., *The Secret Identity of the Beloved Disciple* (Mahwah: Paulist Press, 1992)